# Vegetarian Cuisine

*A unique collection of recipes
from the finest vegetarian restaurants
in Great Britain*

Fontana/Collins

First published in Great Britain by Absolute Press 1982
First issued in Fontana Paperbacks 1984
Second impression December 1984
Third impression August 1985

Copyright © Absolute Press (Publishers) 1982

Editor: Jenny Mann

Set in Linotron Plantin
Made and printed in Great Britain by
William Collins Sons & Co. Ltd, Glasgow

# Vegetarian Cuisine

# Contents

# Introduction

It just seemed a marvellous idea – bring together the finest talents working in the vegetarian restaurant scene in Great Britain and ask them to contribute their favourite recipes for a cookery book. The chefs were approached and, to the delight of the editor, seized on the opportunity to show the world what they could do. A mouthwatering variety of styles and influences abound: Gujerati vegetarian, wholefood, vegan, macrobiotic, Chinese stir-fry, in fact everything that is good in the world of vegetarian cooking.

*Vegetarian Cuisine* does not pretend to offer a nutritionally balanced dietary plan for those wishing to eat vegetarian, many other cookery books deal with such things quite satisfactorily. Vegetarian Cuisine is a delightful pot-pourri of recipes, assembled deliberately to be cooked for when your taste buds desire something a little bit more exotic and special.

The book's format is deliberately simple and straightforward. We don't want the recipes to be lost in a confusion of chapter and sub-chapter headings. There are four sections; salads, starters, main dishes and sweets, enabling the home cook to devise a meal or dinner party with ease.

*Vegetarian Cuisine* is also a very useful guide to the finest vegetarian restaurants. A map of the United Kingdom at the back of the book shows where all the contributing restaurants are to be found, accompanied by a list of addresses and telephone numbers.

*Vegetarian Cuisine* is the product of a group of dedicated and talented chefs, all of whom kindly gave up much of their valuable time to help in contributing to this excellent and original cookery book.

# Salads

## Avocado, Mushroom and Garlic Salad

*Wholemeal Vegetarian Café, Streatham*
*Chef: David Martin*

2 ripe avocados, thickly sliced
1 lb (450g) firm button
   mushrooms, thickly sliced

2 cloves garlic, crushed

*For the dressing:*
1 tablespoon cider or wine
   vinegar
3 tablespoons olive oil
3 tablespoons natural yoghurt

1 teaspoon Dijon mustard
salt and freshly ground black
   pepper

Mix the prepared vegetables together in a large salad bowl.

Combine the ingredients for the dressing and mix together well, adding seasoning to taste.

Pour the dressing over the salad and toss.

# Bean Salad

*Harvest, London*
*Chef: Giuseppe Rossi*

4 oz (125g) kidney beans, cooked
4 oz (125g) haricot beans, cooked
1 onion, finely chopped

5 oz (150g) tin sweetcorn, drained
fresh parsley, chopped

*For the dressing:*
4 tablespoons white wine or vinegar
8 tablespoons corn oil

1 teaspoon mustard
salt and black pepper

Mix all the salad ingredients together in a bowl.

Mix the dressing ingredients together.

Pour the dressing over the salad – add about half the dressing to start with, toss the salad and add more to taste.

---

# Beansprout and Cashew Nut Salad

*Grapevine, Birmingham*
*Chef: Pat Gully*

½ red cabbage, finely chopped
1 cup unsalted cashew nuts

casserole dish full fresh beansprouts

*For the dressing:*
equal quantities sunflower oil, cider vinegar and tamari

2 cloves garlic, crushed

On an ovenproof plate roast the cashew nuts at 200°C/400°F/gas 6 for 5–10 minutes until light brown.

In a salad bowl, mix all the salad ingredients together.

Mix the dressing ingredients together and just before serving pour over salad and dress carefully.

---

# Chunky Beetroot Salad                                  *Serves 4*

*Nature's Way, Eastbourne*
*Chefs: Maurice and Dorothy Fossitt*

12 oz (350g) beetroot, cooked          1 large green apple, unpeeled
2 sticks celery

*For the dressing:*
½ teaspoon vegetable oil          ½ teaspoon cider vinegar

Dice the beetroot, celery and apple into ½"(1cm) cubes. Mix together in a bowl.

Shake the very light dressing together and mix with the salad ingredients until the colours blend a little. Serve chilled on a bed of lettuce.

# Cabbage and Carrot Salad

*York Wholefood Restaurant, York*
*Chef: Peter Graves*

1 lb (450g) cabbage, chopped
   more finely than for cooking
1 large carrot, grated
inside stalks of 1 head celery,
   chopped

½ red pepper, chopped
1–2 courgettes, sliced
juice 1 lemon
good handful sesame seeds
salt

*To vary this salad you could chop an apple into it or make it sweeter by using orange juice instead of the lemon. Add some dried fruit or change the texture by mixing in some grated coconut.*

Put the cabbage in a shallow dish. Salt generously (about a dessertspoonful) and put to one side for 30–60 minutes. The salt will soften the cabbage enough to let it blend with the other ingredients.

Put the celery, pepper and courgettes into a bowl. Put the grated carrot on top and squeeze the lemon juice all over and toss well.

Toast the sesame seeds under the grill until they are just brown and add to the salad.

Mix in the cabbage and season to taste.

# Red Cabbage Salad with Caraway

*The Old Bakehouse, Castle Cary*
*Chef: Susan Roxburgh*

1 small red cabbage, finely
    shredded
2 teaspoons caraway seeds

good French dressing with a little
    garlic

Mix the cabbage with the dressing. Add the caraway seeds, toss and
leave to stand for about 1 hour before serving.

---

# Sweet Cabbage and Wheat Salad      *Serves 4*

*Marno's, Ipswich*
*Chef: Julie*

1 large orange, peeled and
    chopped
1 large apple, cored and
    chopped, but not peeled
1 firm banana, chopped
4 oz (125g) grapes, pipped and
    chopped

4 oz (125g) whole wheat grain,
    cooked until tender
¼ hard white cabbage (about 12
    oz/350g), shredded
2 tablespoons concentrated apple
    juice
large pinch ground allspice

*This is a very summery and refreshing salad and can be made an hour or
so in advance so that the flavours blend together.*

Mix all the fruit with the cabbage.

Mix in the cooled wheat and stir in the apple concentrate. Season with
allspice.

# Caribbean Rice Salad

*Serves 4*

*Cherry Orchard, London*
*Chef: Hilary Swain*

1 lb (450g) cooked brown rice,
 long or short grain
4 bananas, sliced and sprinkled
 with lemon juice
1 red apple, diced and sprinkled
 with lemon juice

bunch grapes, pipped and halved
½ small pineapple, diced
2 tablespoons walnuts, chopped
2 tablespoons coconut
1 leek, finely chopped

*For the dressing:*
½ cup mayonnaise
2 tablespoons lemon juice or
 wine vinegar

pinch salt
½ teaspoon mustard
¼ teaspoon cayenne pepper

To keep the rice grains separate, sauté the uncooked rice in a little hot oil before adding the hot water to cook. Drop in a clove or two and remove after the rice is done.

Combine all the salad ingredients in a large bowl. Stir in the dressing with care. Serve and eat well.

---

# Carrot and Cheese Salad

*Serves 4*

*Henderson's Salad Table, Edinburgh*
*Chef: Janet Henderson*

8 oz (225g) carrots, grated
4 oz (125g) Cheddar cheese,
 grated

2 tomatoes, cut into wedges
1 small onion, finely sliced
cress to garnish

*For the dressing:*
juice 1 lemon

salt and pepper

oregano

¼ pint (150ml) olive oil

Place all the dressing ingredients in a screw top jar and shake well – leave to blend for at least 1 hour.

Mix the carrots, cheese, onion and tomato gently together. Pour over the dressing and garnish with cress.

---

# Carrot, Peanut and Sultana Salad

*Cheese Press, Crickhowell*
*Chef: Mrs Morgan-Grenville*

4 carrots, finely grated

1 tablespoon roasted peanuts

1 tablespoon sultanas or raisins

vinaigrette dressing made with lemon juice and sweetened with honey

Mix together the carrot, peanuts and sultanas. Cover in the vinaigrette and toss well.

---

# Oaty Carrot Salad

*Serves 4–6*

*Marno's, Ipswich*
*Chef: Julie*

1 lb (450g) good quality carrots

8 oz (225g) whole oat groats, soaked in cold water overnight

¼ cucumber, chopped but with the skin left on

4 oz (125g) raisins

4 oz (125g) cashews

juice 1 lemon

mixed herbs to taste

15

Peel the carrots, unless they are very young and clean and then either mince or grate them coarsely.

Drain the oats, which should be quite soft, and add them to the carrot along with the cucumber.

Add the raisins and nuts. Mix in the lemon juice and add a few mixed herbs. In the summer a little finely chopped fresh mint and parsley can be used.

---

# Cauliflower and Banana Salad    *Serves 4*

*Pilgrims, Tunbridge Wells*
*Chef: Rosa Bruce*

1 largish cauliflower, trimmed
    and divided into florets
2 bananas
juice ½ lemon

3 fl. oz (75ml) natural yoghurt
3 fl. oz (75ml) mayonnaise
1 dessertspoon freshly chopped
    parsley or chives

Boil the cauliflower in lightly salted water for about 6 minutes, taking care not to overcook it. Drain, refresh under cold water and set aside.

Slice the bananas and stir with the lemon juice to prevent discolouring.

When the cauliflower is completely cold gently combine all the ingredients. Sprinkle with the parsley or chives and serve immediately.

# Chinese Leaves and Green Pepper

*Good Food Café, Llandrindod Wells*
*Chef: Sue Early*

1 Chinese cabbage, chopped
2 oz (50g) sunflower seeds

1 green pepper, chopped

*For the dressing:*
6 tablespoons olive oil
3 tablespoons lemon juice or
    cider/wine vinegar
1 teaspoon sugar

1 teaspoon mustard powder
2 cloves garlic, crushed
salt and pepper

Toss the salad ingredients in the dressing and serve.

---

# Pressed Chinese Cabbage Salad

*Natural Snack, London*
*Chef: Bretta Carthey*

½ small head Chinese cabbage,
    cut diagonally into 1" strips
1 teaspoon sea salt

1½ tablespoons brown rice
    vinegar or lemon juice

Sprinkle the cabbage with salt and place in a suitable container so that the cabbage can be pressed. Put a plate on top with a weight and leave for at least 30 minutes.

Pour off water and squeeze out any remaining liquid. Rinse the cabbage and toss in the brown rice vinegar or lemon juice.

# Fruity Coleslaw

*Food For Thought, Sherborne*
*Chefs: Michael and Margaret Balfour*

¼ large cabbage, finely chopped
1 large carrot, grated

1 orange
3 oz (75g) seedless raisins

*For the mayonnaise:*
about ½ pint (275ml) sunflower
  oil
1 tablespoon cider vinegar
1 tablespoon lemon juice

1 dessertspoon honey
generous pinch salt
generous pinch mustard

If you fancy a nutty coleslaw, simply substitute the fruit with the nuts of your choice.

To make the mayonnaise, put all the ingredients, except the oil, into a liquidiser and turn on for a few seconds to mix thoroughly. While the liquidiser remains on, add the oil in a gentle, steady stream. As the mayonnaise thickens, oil will start to stay unmixed on the top – in order to thicken thoroughly when this happens, turn off the machine and restart after a few seconds. Repeat until you have a nice, thick mayonnaise.

Chop up the whole orange, including the pith, finely to give a tangy flavour. Mix it into the cabbage, carrot and raisins. Stir in enough mayonnaise to coat the fruit and vegetables evenly.

# Cranks Chunky Salad

*Serves 2–3 keen salad eaters*

*Cranks, London*

1 large head celery, washed and
    chopped into small chunks
1 small red pepper
1 medium apple
juice of 1 lemon

4 oz (125g) cashew nuts, lightly
    roasted
French dressing, made from
    cider vinegar and vegetable oil
parsley, freshly chopped

Cut the red pepper in half and remove the seeds. Wash and slice into
strips. Cut up the apple, core and chop into cubes and then toss in
lemon juice.

Put all the salad ingredients, including the cashew nuts, into a pottery
bowl and toss in the French dressing. Sprinkle the salad with parsley.

---

# The Eighth Day Salad

*Serves 6*

*On the Eighth Day, Manchester*
*Chef: Paul Morrison*

¼ white cabbage, shredded
¼ red cabbage, shredded
½ head celery, chopped
½ cucumber, diced

1 red pepper, diced
1 green pepper, diced
½ punnet beansprouts
1 punnet cress

*For the dressing:*
¼ pint (150ml) sunflower oil
⅛ pint (75ml) cider vinegar
½ teaspoon basil
½ teaspoon paprika
½ teaspoon mustard
sprinkling black pepper

½ small onion
1 small tomato
1 clove garlic
a little honey or apple
    concentrate

Prepare all the salad ingredients and mix together in a large bowl.

Put all the dressing ingredients together in a blender and whizz. It should go thick and creamy. It is possible to use tomato purée instead of the whole tomato but this does not thicken quite so well. Also, try adding a piece of fruit, a banana say, to the dressing mixture.

Pour the dressing over the salad and toss.

---

# Flora's Salad

*Season's Kitchen, Forest Row*
*Chef: Liz Boisseau*

6 small young leeks, finely sliced
4 oz (125g) mushrooms, finely sliced
1 ripe avocado, cubed
4 tomatoes, skinned and cut into wedges

vinaigrette dressing to taste – add a pinch sugar to improve taste
parsley, freshly chopped to garnish

Prepare all the ingredients and toss in the dressing. Garnish with the chopped parsley.

# Mixed Fruit and Vegetable Salad

*Neal's Yard Bakery, London*
*Chef: Rachel Haigh*

¼ cucumber, chopped
¼ punnet beanshoots
1 red pepper, chopped
1 medium parsnip, grated
1 medium carrot, grated
2 small eating apples, chopped

1 medium pear, chopped
2 tablespoons roasted sunflower
 seeds
1 heaped tablespoon raisins or
 dates

*For the dressing:*
zest and juice ½ lemon
½ teaspoon honey
2 tablespoons tamari
2 tablespoons oil

1 clove garlic, crushed
touch root ginger, finely grated
salt and black pepper

*The secret of a good salad is texture, colour and flavour. Any combination of fruits and vegetables can be used and the addition of nuts, seeds and dried fruits increases the nutritional value. Add more or less of any of the ingredients in the salad to preference.*

Mix all the ingredients together.

Make the dressing by putting all the ingredients in a screw top jar and shaking well.

Pour the dressing over the salad and toss 10 minutes before serving.

# Kidney Bean Salad

*Herbs, Skipton*

*Equal quantities of:*

red kidney beans, cooked and
  cooled
mushrooms, sliced

onion, sliced
green pepper, sliced

French dressing
2 tablespoons parsley, chopped

Mix all the vegetables together and put in a bowl. Sprinkle over the parsley, pour on the dressing and toss.

---

# Special Green Salad with Herb Dressing   *Serves 6*

*Good Earth, Wells*
*Chef: Tina Dearling*

½ head Chinese leaves, chopped
½ iceberg lettuce, chopped
¼ large cucumber, diced
1 ripe avocado pear, sliced
1 bunch watercress, chopped
1 green pepper, seeded and sliced

2 apples, chopped
1 pear, chopped
1 box cress
1 bunch parsley, finely chopped
2 hard-boiled eggs, chopped

*For the dressing:*

¼ pint (150ml) mayonnaise
1 small carton natural yoghurt
good pinch English mustard
1 clove garlic, crushed

1 teaspoon each of dill, chives,
  thyme and marjoram
salt and black pepper

Liquidise all the dressing ingredients together.

Mix all the prepared salad ingredients together with dressing.

# Brown Lentil Salad

*Good Food Cafe, Llandrindod Wells*
*Chef: Sue Early*

8 oz (225g) brown lentils, cooked
    until soft but unbroken
1 onion, chopped, or 4 spring
    onions, chopped

4 tomatoes, diced
2 cloves garlic, crushed
salt and pepper

*For the dressing:*
6 tablespoons olive oil
3 tablespoons lemon juice
1 teaspoon sugar

1 teaspoon mustard powder
salt and pepper

Toss the salad ingredients in the dressing and serve.

---

# Marguerite Salad

*Slenders, London*
*Chef: Michael O'Sullivan*

1 head celery
2 bunches watercress
3 oz (75g) raisins
3 eating apples

juice 1 lemon
8 fl. oz (225g) natural yoghurt
seasoning to taste

Wash the celery, watercress, raisins and apples.

Slice the celery into small pieces.

Cut the excess stalk from the watercress.

Core and slice the apples into small pieces. Add the lemon juice and raisins.

Mix all the ingredients in a bowl, season and mix in the natural yoghurt.

---

# Marinated Mushrooms with Green Salad

*Harvest, Ambleside*
*Chef: Gillian Kelly*

1 lb (450g) smooth, firm button-
   shaped mushrooms

*For the marinade:*

½ cup olive oil

juice 1 lemon

2 tablespoons parsley, freshly
   chopped

2 cloves garlic, crushed

½ small red pepper, grated

salt and black pepper

crisp green lettuce

cucumber, sliced

watercress

chopped or sliced hard-boiled
   egg to garnish

parsley to garnish

Make up the marinade by mixing all the ingredients together. Stir in the mushrooms and leave for several hours, mixing them occasionally so that all the mushrooms are well coated in the marinade. Take care not to damage any when stirring.

Serve the mushrooms piled up in a glistening mound on a bed of crisp green lettuce, cucumber, watercress and garnished with the chopped egg and fresh parsley.

# Mixed Vegetable Salad with French Mustard and Herb Dressing

*Nuthouse, London*
*Chefs: Magdi Aboulnass and Abraham Nasr*

3 carrots, sliced
½ green cabbage, shredded
½ white cabbage, shredded
½ head celery, sliced

½ cucumber, sliced
1 medium-sized beetroot, grated
few beansprouts

*For the dressing:*
4 teaspoons French mustard
4 tablespoons white white
   vinegar
2 cloves garlic, crushed
1 small onion

¼ teaspoon curry powder
1 tablespoon (or more) mixed
   herbs, freshly chopped
8–10 tablespoons sunflower oil

Combine all the prepared vegetables together until evenly mixed.

Place all the ingredients for the dressing, except the oil, in a liquidiser and blend until they form a thick, heavy liquid. Gradually dribble in the oil and mix it in well. Taste and adjust seasoning. Pour over the salad and toss.

# Summer Mixed Salad

*Healthy, Wealthy and Wise, London*
*Chef: Lina*

5 radishes, finely sliced
¼ cucumber, finely sliced
1–2 sticks, celery, chopped
½ green pepper, chopped
1½ tablespoons cashew nuts
1½ tablespoons hazel, walnuts or
    peanuts
handful sprouted mung or lentils
handful parsley, freshly chopped

2 crisp sweet tomatoes, chopped
4–8 black olives
1 cooked potato, chopped
    (optional)
1 carrot, grated (optional)
1 lettuce – use an equal
    proportion to the rest of the
    ingredients when mixed
    together

*For the dressing:*
3 tablespoons fresh lemon juice
½ teaspoon French mustard
6 tablespoons olive oil
1 teaspoon oregano
1 teaspoon honey

½ teaspoon salt
¼ teaspoon pepper
1 teaspoon fresh basil
¼ teaspoon fresh thyme

Combine all the salad dressing ingredients together and mix well.

Prepare all the ingredients, ending up with the lettuce, and mix them together gently.

Pour over the dressing and toss just before serving.

# Mixed Winter Salad

*Ganesha, Axminster*
*Chefs: Fred and Penny Easton*

½ Chinese cabbage
1 bunch watercress or 1 punnet
  cress
1 green pepper, seeded and sliced
2 stalks celery, cut diagonally
  into thin slices
2 oz (50g) mushrooms, sliced
  thinly
4 tomatoes, chopped into
  quarters or eighths depending
  on size

1 medium carrot, cut diagonally
  into thin slices
4 oz (125g) frozen sweetcorn (off
  the cob)
1 avocado pear (optional)
12 black olives (optional)

*For the dressing:*
2 cloves garlic, crushed
salt and black pepper
1½ fl. oz (40ml) cider vinegar

1½ fl. oz (40ml) lemon juice
3 fl. oz (75ml) sunflower oil
3 fl. oz (75ml) virgin olive oil

Cut the Chinese cabbage in half and then quarters lengthwise and slice thinly across.

Break the watercress up if the stalks are too thick.

Cook and drain the corn.

Quarter the peeled avocado lengthwise and slice across on a slight diagonal.

Mix everything together carefully, so that nothing breaks up.

Mix the dressing ingredients together well and pour as much or as little as you like over the salad. Toss. Keep the leftover dressing in the fridge in an airtight jar.

# Oriental Coleslaw

*Mother Nature, Stroud*
*Chef: Cindy*

1 Chinese cabbage, sliced sideways in rings
2 large carrots, finely grated

½ green pepper, thinly sliced in rings

*For the dressing:*
4 fl. oz (125ml) tamari
4 fl. oz (125ml) wine vinegar

2 tablespoons brown sugar

Mix the cabbage, carrot and pepper together in a bowl.

Make up dressing by combining the tamari, wine vinegar and brown sugar together.

Pour some of the dressing over the salad, toss and then add more to taste.

---

# Rice and Peanut Salad

*Serves 4–6*

*Siop Y Chwarel (The Quarry Shop), Machynlleth*
*Chef: Ann Watson*

8 oz (225g) brown long grain rice
8 oz (225g) peanuts
1 large onion, finely chopped

ground black pepper
tamari, to taste
oil for frying

Boil the rice until tender, about 30 minutes. Strain, rinse and leave to cool.

Fry the peanuts gently in some oil for 15 minutes until softened. Add the tamari and increase the heat, cooking for a further 10 minutes – this will make a lot of noise but don't panic.

Add the peanuts, more tamari if desired, the onion and black pepper to the cooked rice. Mix and leave to cool.

---

## Brown Rice and Toasted Hazelnut Salad

*Food For Thought, London*
*Chef: Siriporn Duncan*

3–4 cups brown short-grain rice,
  cooked
1 cup toasted hazelnuts
1 cup parsley, chopped

½ cup sesame seeds, toasted
6–8 spring onions, chopped into
  ½" pieces

*For the dressing:*
3 tablespoons oil
1 tablespoon tamari or soya sauce
juice ½ lemon

salt to taste
1 tablespoon crunchy peanut
  butter

Combine all the ingredients for the salad.

Blend together all the ingredients for the dressing apart from the peanut butter which is added once the other ingredients are well mixed.

Pour the dressing over the salad, mix well and leave to stand in a cool place for about 30 minutes before serving.

# Scarlet Salad

*Gannets, Newark*
*Chef: Hilary Bower*

1 lb (450g) red cabbage,
   shredded
2 large carrots, coarsely grated

4 beetroots, cooked and diced
1 box cress

*For the garlic dressing:*
6 tablespoons vegetable oil
3 tablespoons red wine vinegar
1 teaspoon sugar

1 clove garlic
pinch dried mustard
salt and pepper

Mix all the salad ingredients together.

Whisk all the dressing ingredients together and pour over the salad.
Toss well and allow 30 minutes before serving to let all the flavours
blend.

---

# Spinach, Cauliflower and Sesame Salad

*Delany's, Shrewsbury*
*Chefs: Odette and Belinda*

1 colander of spinach or chard
1 small cauliflower
4 oz (125g) sesame seeds

juice 1 lemon
salt

*For the dressing:*
4 parts olive oil
1 part wine vinegar
salt and black pepper

whole grain French mustard to
   taste

Break the cauliflower into pieces and cook in very little water until barely tender. Or use raw in smaller pieces.

Wash the spinach or chard and tear up. Put into a salad bowl.

Toast the sesame seeds in a dry frying pan, stirring them and watching them carefully lest they burn.

Mix the cauliflower and sesame seeds with the spinach. Add salt and lemon juice to taste.

Mix all the dressing ingredients together and pour over the salad. Toss.

---

# Tabouli

*Huckleberry's, Bath*
*Chef: Sarah Jinks*

1 cup bulgar wheat
1½–2 cups boiling water
1 teaspoon salt
juice 2 lemons
4 tomatoes, chopped up small
1 small bunch parsley, finely
    chopped

small bunch spring onions, finely
    chopped
3 cloves garlic, chopped
1 tablespoon oil
salt and black pepper

Place the bulgar in a saucepan with a tight fitting lid. Season with salt and pepper. Add the boiling water and lemon juice – the bulgar should be covered by ½″ (1cm) of liquid.

Leave in a warm place until the bulgar is cooked and dry.

Add all the other ingredients and mix thoroughly. Check seasoning – you may like to add more lemon juice.

# Three of a Kind

*Country Kitchen, Southsea*
*Chef: Sue Reynolds*

*For the Rice Salad:*

8 oz (225g) brown rice, boiled, rinsed in cold water and drained

1 small green pepper, finely chopped

2 mushrooms, finely chopped

3 small tomatoes, skinned and chopped

black pepper

2 tablespoons olive oil

¼ teaspoon cumin

2 pinches chilli powder

1 tablespoon tomato purée

*For the Bean Salad*

1 lb (450g) mixed red kidney beans, pintos and chick peas

3 small tomatoes, blanched, peeled and chopped

black pepper

3 tablespoons olive oil

2 cloves garlic, crushed

¼ onion, finely chopped

2 pinches curry powder

2 oz (50g) bean shoots, washed and drained

*For the Carrot Salad:*

6–8 large carrots, washed and grated

¼ small fresh fennel, finely chopped

2 oz (50g) beanshoots, washed and drained

freshly ground black pepper

2 tablespoons olive oil

4 mushrooms, finely chopped

To make the rice salad, mix the pepper and mushrooms with the rice. In a separate bowl put the tomatoes, a good sprinkling of black pepper, cumin, chilli powder and purée and mix well. Fold into the rice with a wooden spoon until the rice is an even pink colour with no white patches.

For the bean salad, soak the beans, chick peas and pintos overnight. Drain, cover with boiling water and boil for 45 minutes. Stir occasionally with a wooden spoon but do not damage the beans. Cool under cold running water and leave to drain in a colander. In a bowl, put the potatoes, black pepper, olive oil, garlic, onion and curry powder. Mix well. Using a wooden spoon, fold in the beanshoots, taking care not to damage any but making sure they are well mixed.

For the carrot salad, add the fennel, beanshoots, a liberal sprinkling black pepper and the olive oil to the grated carrot. Fold together carefully with the mushrooms.

Serve these three salads together in individual bowls.

---

# Waldorf Salad

*Food For Health, London*
*Chef: Abdel Rahman*

2 good tablespoons home made
  mayonnaise
1 head celery, sliced or 1 medium
  celeriac, grated
2 oz (50g) walnuts, chopped
3 oz (75g) dates, chopped

3 bananas, sliced
4 medium apples, sliced or
  grated
cider vinegar or lemon juice if
  required
brown sugar, if required

*All the measurements for this salad are optional and can easily be altered to suit individual taste.*

Place the mayonnaise in a bowl large enough to allow for mixing all the ingredients with ease.

Mix the celery into the mayonnaise to prevent browning. Add the walnuts, dates, banana and apple, mixing well between each addition. If the mixture is too dry add more mayonnaise.

Leave covered for 1 hour and then taste. If too sweet add a little vinegar or lemon juice or if too sharp add a few more dates or brown sugar. If you can achieve this 'sweet-sour' balance you will have made a delightful salad – cooking apples can be useful for this purpose.

Serve with a green salad and cottage cheese.

---

# Hockneys Waldorf with Orange Mayonnaise

*Hockneys, Croydon*
*Chef: Paul Melia*

6 oz (175g) assorted roasted nuts, broken up
8 oz (225g) cheese, diced

4 medium apples, diced
4 oz (125g) dates, chopped
1 large head celery, chopped

*For the orange mayonnaise dressing:*
2 eggs
½ pint (275ml) salad oil
2 dessertspoons vinegar
1 teaspoon mustard

salt and black pepper
4 oz (125g) cottage cheese
juice and zest 1½ oranges

Mix all the salad ingredients together carefully.

To make the dressing, put all the ingredients, except the oil, cottage cheese and orange juice and rind, into a liquidiser and run at full speed. Slowly drizzle in the oil until the mixture emulsifies.

Mix in the cottage cheese and orange juice and zest.

Pour over the salad and mix in. Chill and serve. You will find that any leftover dressing will keep in the fridge for 2–3 days.

# Watercress and Mushroom Salad

*Serves 4*

*Super Natural, Newcastle upon Tyne*
*Chef: James Leitch*

4 oz (125g) mushrooms
juice 1 lemon
½ teaspoon salt
2 bunches watercress, trimmed
   and coarsely chopped

1 medium onion, finely sliced
vinaigrette dressing or
   mayonnaise

Wash the mushrooms and place them in a pan with a cupful of cold water. Add the lemon juice and salt. Bring to the boil, then cool immediately by placing the pan under a cold running tap. When the mushrooms are cold, chop them up roughly.

Place the mushrooms, watercress and sliced onions in a suitable bowl and mix gently with sufficient vinaigrette dressing or mayonnaise to coat the watercress.

---

# Wheat Salad

*Serves 4*

*Clinchs Salad House, Chichester*
*Chef: Mrs A. Ellis*

6 oz (175g) uncooked wheat,
   soaked in water overnight
2 oz (50g) peanuts, chopped
2 oz (50g) dates, chopped
3 oz (75g) mixed red and green
   pepper, chopped

seasoning to taste
watercress
3 tablespoons vinaigrette
   dressing

In clean water put the soaked wheat, add a little salt and cook at 15 lb pressure in a pressure cooker for 6 minutes, or in an open saucepan until done. Drain.

Add the peppers, nuts and dates to the drained wheat.

Stir in the vinaigrette dressing, seasoning and a few finely chopped herbs if desired.

Pile into a bowl and surround with sprigs of watercress.

# Starters

## Imperial Almond Soup

*Serves 4*

*Food For Thought, London*
*Chef: Siriporn Duncan*

1 small onion, finely chopped
2 tablespoons corn oil
2 sticks celery, finely chopped
1 tablespoon toasted almonds
1 teaspoon sultanas, pre-soaked
⅓ cup brown rice, cooked
1½ pints (875ml) vegetable stock

1 teaspoon grated lemon rind
2 egg yolks, beaten well
fresh lemon juice to taste
salt, black pepper and sugar to taste
2 tablespoons spring onions
parsley, finely chopped

Sauté the onions in the oil. When slightly browned and soft add the celery, almonds, sultanas and rice. Stir-cook for 4 minutes. Add the stock, bring to the boil and simmer until all the ingredients are quite soft.

Stir in the lemon rind, remove from heat and allow to cool for a couple of minutes. Slowly add the beaten egg yolks, stirring briskly all the time to prevent the eggs becoming lumpy – a hand whisk works well. Season with lemon juice, salt, pepper and a very little brown sugar if desired.

Garnish with spring onions and parsley and serve very hot.

# Carrot and Coriander Soup

Serves 4

*Good Earth, Wells*
*Chef: Tina Dearling*

1 lb (450g) carrots, peeled and chopped
2 onions, chopped
1 oz (50g) butter
1 tablespoon 81% wheatmeal flour

1 pint (575ml) milk
juice and rind of ½ lemon
1 teaspoon mixed herbs
2 teaspoons coriander
cream to garnish
little fat for frying

Sauté the carrots and onions in a little fat until tender.

Make a white sauce by cooking the flour and butter in a saucepan for 2–3 minutes. Add the milk and stir until it thickens. Add the juice and rind of the lemon and the mixed herbs and coriander.

Liquidise the carrots and onions and mix with the sauce. Heat through.

Serve hot finished with a swirl of cream.

---

# Carrot and Onion Soup

Serves 4

*Nature's Way, Eastbourne*
*Chefs: Maurice and Dorothy Fossit*

8 oz (225g) onions, chopped

8 oz (225g) carrots, thinly sliced

*For the stock:*
1 vegetable stock cube
½ teaspoon barmene

1 pint (575ml) water

sea salt and black pepper

croûtons to decorate

Mix together the stock ingredients.

Pressure cook the carrots for 3 minutes. Add the onions and pressure cook for a further 3 minutes. Pour the vegetables and juices into an electric mixer and blend.

Add the stock to the puréed vegetables and re-heat in a pan. Add the seasoning to taste and serve hot with the croûtons.

---

# Cauliflower Soup                                      *Serves 4*

*Super Natural, Newcastle upon Tyne*
*Chef: James Leitch*

1 large cauliflower, washed and trimmed
   12 oz (350g) old potatoes, peeled and quartered
2½ pints (1¼ litres) milk

1½ oz (40g) butter
pinch nutmeg
salt and pepper
Grated carrot and chopped chervil to garnish

Put 2 pints (generous litre) of milk in a pan and add the cauliflower and potatoes. Bring to the boil, add the seasoning and simmer until the potatoes are cooked, about 25 minutes.

Sieve or blend the milk mixture and return to the pan. Add the remaining milk, a pinch of nutmeg and adjust the seasoning. Bring to the boil and add the butter in small pieces. Serve immediately sprinkled with the carrot and chervil.

# Cucumber and Celery Soup

*Serves 6*

*Grapevine, Birmingham*
*Chef: Pat Gully*

1 cucumber, peeled and finely
   chopped
1 head of celery, roughly
   chopped
½ head of Chinese leaves,
   chopped

fresh mint to taste
sea salt
8 oz (225g) natural yoghurt
sunflower oil

Sauté the cucumber, celery and Chinese leaves in the sunflower oil until soft.

Add enough water to cover the vegetables and add the mint and sea salt to taste. Allow to simmer for 10–15 minutes then mix in the natural yoghurt.

Liquidise the soup until smooth, return to the pan and adjust seasoning.

You can serve this very versatile soup either hot or chilled, garnished with mint or cucumber rings.

---

# Leek Soup

*Serves 4*

*Cranks, London*

1 small onion, finely chopped
2 leeks, very finely sliced using
   green leaves as well as
   blanched
1 carrot, finely diced

1 tablespoon thick cream
pepper and salt
knob butter
1½ pints (875ml) vegetable stock

Fry the onion and leeks in the melted butter – do not allow to brown.

Add stock and carrots and simmer until tender.

Blend, retaining a small amount of carrot to toss back into the pale green blended soup to give a dash of colour. At the very last moment before serving, add a tablespoon of thick cream.

---

# Lentil and Green Pepper Soup       *Serves 4*

*Healthy, Wealthy and Wise, London*
*Chef: Kath*

6 oz (175g) red lentils
2 pints (generous litre) vegetable
  stock
3 green peppers, seeded and
  roughly chopped
few bay leaves
½ teaspoon coriander

1 teaspoon cumin
½ teaspoon turmeric
pinch asofoetida
salt and pepper
1 tablespoon tomato purée
tamari to taste

Wash the lentils and place them in a large pan with the stock, green peppers, bay leaves, spices and seasoning. Bring to the boil and simmer covered until the lentils are soft, about 20–30 minutes.

Add the tamari and tomato purée to taste and purée all the ingredients. Return to a clean saucepan, adjust the seasoning and serve.

# Minestrone

*Harvest, London*
*Chef: Giuseppe Rossi*

2 oz (50g) margarine
1 small onion, chopped
1 clove garlic
½ head celery, chopped
¼ head white cabbage, chopped
1 carrot, chopped
2 courgettes, chopped
1 medium potato, diced
2 pints (generous litre) vegetable
   stock
2 bay leaves
sprinkling rosemary

14 oz (400g) tin tomatoes
2 tablespoons tomato purée
4 oz (125g) cooked haricot or
   kidney beans
4 oz (125g) peas
4 oz (125g) macaroni
salt and black pepper
pinch oregano
parsley, freshly chopped to
   garnish
Parmesan cheese, to garnish

Melt the margarine in your largest pan and add the onion, garlic, celery, cabbage, courgettes and potatoes. Sauté for about 10 minutes until soft, stirring from time to time to ensure all cooks evenly.

Add the stock, bay leaves and rosemary. Cover the pan and simmer for 15 minutes.

Add the tomatoes, tomato purée, beans, peas and macaroni. Season with salt, pepper and oregano and simmer for a further 30 minutes.

Remove the bay leaves and serve the soup very hot. Sprinkle each portion with the parsley and Parmesan.

# Miso Soup

*Natural Snack, London*
*Chef: Bretta Carthey*

1 handful wakame sea vegetable, thinly sliced and soaked in water
5 cups vegetable stock or water
2 cups leeks, thinly sliced

6 oz (175g) tofu, cut into small cubes
2 tablespoons genmai or mugi miso
spring onions, chopped

Bring the stock to the boil. Add the wakame and soaking water and bring back to the boil. Lower the heat and simmer gently for a few minutes.

Add the leeks and simmer for a further 5 minutes. Add the tofu and simmer for 5 more minutes.

Take a small amount of liquid from the soup and add to the miso to make a paste. Stir it into the soup and simmer for 2–3 minutes making sure the soup does not boil. Serve garnished with the spring onions.

---

# Split Pea and Potato Soup                    *Serves 4*

*Nettles, Cambridge*
*Chef: Mary Ann Marks*

12 oz (350g) yellow split peas
2 onions, finely chopped
1 clove garlic, crushed
3 potatoes, diced
1 carrot, diced
2 fl. oz (50ml) shoyu or less to taste

1 teaspoon cumin
1 teaspoon coriander
salt and pepper
1½ pints (scant litre) water
oil for frying

Boil the split peas in a pan of water until soft.

Fry the onion, garlic, potato and carrot until tender.

Add the cumin, coriander and salt and pepper and then the water, split peas and shoyu to taste. Heat together and serve.

---

## Toasted Sunflower and Onion Soup     *Serves 4*

*Wholemeal Vegetarian Café, Streatham*
*Chef: David Martin*

2 large onions, finely chopped
4 oz (125g) 81% wheatmeal
   flour
1 tablespoon soya sauce

2 pints (generous litre) vegetable
   stock
3 oz (85g) sunflower seeds
2 tablespoons oil

Put the sunflower seeds and flour on separate baking trays in the oven and bake until the seeds are crunchy and the flour is just golden.

Sauté the onion until soft. Add the flour and stirring continuously cook this roux for 2–3 minutes. Off the heat add the vegetable stock and the soya sauce and cook until it thickens, stirring all the time.

Grind the sunflower seeds (a clean coffee grinder works well) until they are lightly broken up. Sprinkle them into the soup. Cover the pan and simmer for 40 minutes. Season with salt, pepper and more soya sauce as required. Serve hot.

# Tomato, Cumin and Lentil Soup

*Serves 4*

*Harvest, Ambleside*
*Chef: Steve Muscutt*

1 large onion, chopped
4 oz (125g) red split lentils
4 tablespoons tomato purée and
   1½ pints (scant litre) water or
   1 pint (575ml) tomato juice
   and ½ pint (275ml) water

salt and black pepper
¼ teaspoon cumin (more or less
   to taste)
little oil for cooking
2 tablespoons tamari or shoyu

*This soup is very simple to make but is extremely good and is more popular
with our customers than almost any other we do.*

Gently sauté the onion in a little oil until transparent. Add the lentils
and sauté for a couple of minutes more.

Add the liquid and seasoning. Bring to the boil, then reduce the heat
and cook for a further 20 minutes, stirring frequently to prevent
sticking. Add more liquid if necessary. Stir in tamari a few minutes
before serving. Serve piping hot.

# Tomato and Orange Soup

*Clinchs Salad House, Chichester*
*Chef: Mrs A. Ellis*

1 small onion, finely chopped
1 oz (25g) butter and
   1 tablespoon oil
1 tablespoon parsley, chopped
1 tablespoon celery, chopped
14 oz (400g) tin tomatoes and 2
   fresh tomatoes, skinned
¼ pint (150ml) water
¼ pint (150ml) fresh orange juice

1 heaped tablespoon tomato
   purée
rind from ½ small orange, finely
   grated
small bay leaf
fresh thyme
fresh basil or parsley to garnish,
   finely chopped
salt and pepper

Sauté the onion and celery in oil and butter until soft but not brown. Add the flour and purée and stir well. Cook for a few minutes.

Add water and orange juice, stirring until smooth. Add the tin of tomatoes and the 2 fresh ones. Add seasoning, bay leaf, thyme and parsley. Simmer gently for at least 30 minutes, stirring occasionally to make sure it is not sticking. If the soup seems too thick dilute with more water or orange juice.

Remove bay leaf and liquidise. Return to a clean pan. Add the grated orange rind being careful only to use the zest otherwise the soup will be bitter. Taste and season if necessary – sometimes a little sugar can be added if the tomatoes are a little acid.

If serving hot, sprinkle with parsley. In the summer this soup is lovely served well chilled and sprinkled with fresh basil.

# Aubergine and Curd Cheese Pâté

*Serves 4*

*Huckleberry's, Bath*
*Chef: Judi Macdonald*

2 medium sized aubergines
1 small onion, finely chopped
2 cloves garlic, crushed
2 tablespoons tomato purée
8 oz (225g) curd cheese

juice 1 lemon
vegetable oil
salt and black pepper
parsley to garnish

Preheat oven to 200°C/400°F/gas mark 6.

Top and tail the aubergines and wrap in foil. Bake until soft, about 30 minutes.

Cook the onion and garlic gently in a little vegetable oil until soft.

Skin and roughly chop the aubergines. Purée in a blender with the cheese, tomato purée and lemon juice. Add the onions and garlic and continue to whizz.

When smooth, season to taste and chill. Serve in ramekins, garnished with parsley.

# Black Eyed Bean Pâté

*On The Eighth Day, Manchester*
*Chefs: John Leverton*

Serves 4

8 oz (225g) black eyed beans
2 fl. oz (50ml) 'cold pressed' olive oil
1 fl. oz (25ml) cider vinegar
1–2 cloves garlic, peeled

1 level dessertspoon mint, freshly chopped
1 level teaspoon salt
¼ teaspoon freshly ground black pepper

*This is a particularly versatile mixture which can also be used as a pie filling or as a spread for bread or toast. It can also be turned into rissoles. The dessertspoon of mint can be substituted for a small tin of tomato purée and a teaspoon of basil to give a quite differently flavoured dish.*

Place the beans in a pan of water and boil until soft, about 45 minutes.

Put all the other ingredients into a blender and whizz.

Drain the beans and mash them. Add to the blended ingredients and mix thoroughly. Allow to cool before serving.

---

# Butter Bean Pâté

Serves 4

*Ganesha, Axminster*
*Chefs: Penny and Fred Easton*

8 oz (225g) butter beans, soaked overnight
juice 1 lemon
4 pinches crystal or sea salt and black pepper

2 cloves garlic, crushed
2 teaspoons virgin olive oil
ground coriander, to taste
parsley, freshly chopped

*This was discovered when we ran out of chick peas! A lovely fresh taste. The coriander gives an unusual fragrance to the dish.*

Cook the butter beans until tender (10 minutes in a pressure cooker). Drain and put in a blender with the lemon juice, salt, pepper and garlic. Blend or mash well. Stir in the olive oil.

Turn into a serving dish and sprinkle with the ground coriander and garnish with parsley.

Serve on rye biscuits or Melba toast.

---

# Egg and Sage Pâté                    *Serves 4*

*Herbs, Skipton*

| | |
|---|---|
| 2 hard boiled eggs | 1 teaspoon fresh sage |
| 8 oz (225g) cottage cheese | salt and pepper |
| 1 oz (25g) butter or good margarine | 1–2 tablespoons cream |

Mix all the ingredients together in a Magi-mix or blender. Adjust seasoning and add a little more cream if necessary to give the mixture a spreading consistency.

Pile the pâté into a shallow dish and rough up the top.

Serve with crusty brown bread or crisp biscuits.

# Mushroom and Onion Pâté

*Serves 8*

*Country Kitchen, Southsea*
*Chef: Jean Piper*

1 lb (450g) mushrooms (some shops will sell stalks only)
1 large onion, peeled and chopped
2 oz (50g) butter
1 egg
8 oz (225g) wholemeal breadcrumbs
2 tablespoons milk powder
4 oz (125g) milled mixed nuts
1 teaspoon yeast extract
1 teaspoon mixed herbs
1 teaspoon parsley, freshly chopped
½ teaspoon salt

Chop up the mushrooms roughly or finely, depending on how you prefer the texture of your pâté. Sauté in the butter with the onions until tender.

Add all the other ingredients and mix them together well. Season to taste.

Press the pâté into an ovenproof dish and cover with foil.

Bake at 180°C/350°F/gas 4 for about 1 hour.

Remove from the oven and allow to cool in the tin. Turn out to serve.

# Red Bean Pâté

*Cherry Orchard, London*
*Chef: Teresa Fisher*

8 oz (225g) red kidney beans,
  soaked overnight
1 large Spanish onion, finely
  chopped
2 stalks celery, finely chopped
6 oz (175g) mushrooms, finely
  chopped
2 tablespoons soya oil

1½ oz (35g) butter
2 cloves garlic, crushed
good pinch marjoram, rosemary
  and sage
½ flat teaspoon chilli powder
1 dessertspoon miso paste
salt
24 olives, stoned and halved

Cook the beans until soft. When soft either blend or mash with a potato-masher.

Heat the oil and sauté the onion and celery. After 10–15 minutes add the herbs, chilli powder and garlic. Sauté for another 5 minutes or so, stirring every now and then.

In another pan, melt the butter and sauté the finely chopped mushrooms adding 2 good pinches salt.

Add the mushroom mixture and the onion mixture to the beans. Stir in 1 dessertspoon miso, mixed to a paste with a little water. Blend again, making sure that the mixture does not become too wet. De-stone and halve the olives and mix them well into the pâté.

Take the bowl or dish in which you are going to serve the pâté and spread a little oil mixed with crushed garlic and fresh herbs around the inside. Put in the mixture and pat down well. Chill in the fridge.

Serve decorated with fresh parsley and finely chopped mushrooms or olives. Accompany this excellent pâté with a green salad and finely sliced, toasted wholewheat bread.

# Vegetable Pâté

*Neal's Yard Bakery, London*
*Chef: Rachel Haigh*

2 tablespoons oil
1 small onion, finely chopped
1 small green pepper, finely
    chopped
4 medium sized mushrooms
2 tablespoons coconut
2 tablespoons tamari
2 medium sized tomatoes,
    chopped

½ teaspoon cumin
½ teaspoon coriander
½ teaspoon curry powder
½ teaspoon cardamom
2 cloves garlic, crushed
4 oz (125g) cooked beans, lentils,
    grains or pulses
rings of red pepper, lemon slices
    and parsley to garnish

*Vegetable pâtés are very quick and economical to make and are an excellent way of using up any leftover vegetables, grains, beans or pulses – the choice is up to you.*

Fry the onion and green pepper in the oil with the spices.

Add the coconut and tamari and then the rest of the ingredients, apart from the beans, and fry gently until all the vegetables are tender.

Put the mixture into a blender and mix well – if you do not have a blender, a potato masher will do. Add the beans and blend again until a soft pâté is formed. Adjust the seasoning to taste. The pâté will stiffen slightly as it cools.

Put the pâté into individual ramekins or bowls and decorate the top with rings of red pepper, lemon and the parsley. Serve with hot crusty wholewheat rolls.

# Hummus

*Pilgrims, Tunbridge Wells*
*Chef: Rosa Bruce*

8 oz (225g) chick peas, soaked
   overnight
juice 1 large lemon
1–2 cloves garlic, crushed
5 tablespoons olive oil
5 tablespoons tahini

1 teaspoon sea salt
pinch cayenne
1 tablespoon olive oil, to garnish
sliced lemon, to garnish
paprika, to garnish

Pick over the chick peas carefully, removing any stones and wash thoroughly before soaking overnight, allowing plenty of extra water for expansion.

Cook the chick peas in plenty of unsalted water for 1–2 hours or until tender. Press through a coarse sieve or mouli or liquidise. Reserve a little of the cooking liquid.

Beat the remaining ingredients into the chick peas to make a rich, light cream. If the mixture is too dense it may be thinned with a little of the cooking liquid.

Pile into a bowl and trickle over 1 tablespoon olive oil, dust with paprika and garnish with the sliced lemon. Serve with toasted pitta bread and a green salad.

# Artichoke Soufflé

*Cheese Press, Crickhowell*
*Chef: Mrs Morgan-Grenville*

1½ lb (675g) Jerusalem
   artichokes
1 pint (575ml) mixed milk and
   water
2 eggs

1 oz (25g) Parmesan cheese
salt and black pepper
2 tablespoons breadcrumbs
1 oz (25g) butter

Peel the artichokes and simmer until soft in the milk and water – if you are not stewing the artichokes immediately, leave them in a bowl with the juice of a lemon added.

Drain the artichokes, reserving some of the liquid. Sieve or whizz in a food processor. Season.

Add the beaten egg yolks and enough of the stewing liquid to make a loose mixture.

Beat the egg whites stiffly and fold them into the artichoke mixture.

Place the mixture in a pie dish. Mix the cheese and breadcrumbs together, sprinkle over the top and dot with knobs of butter. Bake at 230°C/450°F/gas 8 for about 20 minutes until the top is browning and set.

# Avocado and Cottage Cheese

*Serves 4*

*Henderson's Salad Table, Edinburgh*
*Chef: Janet Henderson*

2 medium-sized ripe avocados
5 oz (150g) smooth cottage
  cheese
1 clove garlic, crushed

juice 1 lemon
salt and black pepper
pinch mustard
lemon, to decorate

Halve the avocados and remove the stones. Scoop out the flesh and finely mash it. Retain the avocado skins.

Mix the avocado with rest of the ingredients and spoon back into the skins. For the best results mix the ingredients in a blender or food processor.

Garnish each portion with a slice of lemon and freshly ground black pepper.

---

# Avocado and Orange Starter

*Serves 4*

*Mother Nature, Stroud*
*Chef: Cindy*

2 medium sized avocados
2 Jaffa oranges, seedless and thin
  skinned variety

sprig fresh parsley

*For the dressing:*
2 tablespoons sesame or
  sunflower oil
1 tablespoon wine vinegar
2 tablespoons tamari

1 teaspoon brown sugar
pinch salt and freshly ground
  black pepper

Cut avocados in half lengthwise and remove stone. Using a melon baller scoop out the avocado and divide between four small bowls.

Slice a small piece from the tops and bottoms of the oranges. Starting at the top with a sharp knife, work downwards removing the skin and pith in one stroke. Remove all the skin in this way until you have bared all the flesh! Then cut into segments or round slices and arrange in the bowls with the avocados.

Put all the ingredients for the dressing in a small jar and give it a good shake. Add 1 tablespoon of the dressing to each bowl and sprinkle with a little chopped parsley.

---

# Cashew Nut and Spinach Quiche    *Serves 6*

*Slenders, London*
*Chef: Michael O'Sullivan*

*For the pastry:*
6 oz (175g) wholewheat flour          water to mix
3 oz (75g) margarine

3 oz (75g) butter                     nutmeg, grated
½ small onion, chopped                salt
1 clove garlic, chopped               3 eggs
1 lb (450g) fresh cooked spinach      7 fl. oz (200ml) milk
4 oz (125g) cashew nuts, roasted      3 oz (75g) cheese, grated

Make the pastry by rubbing the margarine into the flour well. Add enough water to make a stiff dough. Line a 10″ (26cm) flan case, prick the base and cook for 15–20 minutes at 190°C/375°F/gas 5.

Melt the butter in a pan and add the onions and garlic and cook for a few minutes. Mix in the spinach and cashew nuts. Add the salt and nutmeg and sauté for 5 minutes. Drain off the excess liquid.

Place the filling in the flan case.

Break the eggs into a bowl, add and whisk together. Pour the mixture into the flan case and sprinkle the grated cheese on top. Bake at 180°C/350°F/gas 4 for about 35 minutes.

---

# Courgettes with Rosemary

Serves 4

*Gannets, Newark*
*Chef: Hilary Bower*

1 lb (450g) courgettes, chopped
1 small tin tomatoes
1 medium onion, roughly
    chopped
1 clove garlic, crushed
2 level tablespoons tomato purée

1 teaspoon sugar
1 oz (25g) fresh breadcrumbs
1 oz (25g) Parmesan cheese
1 sprig fresh rosemary
salt and freshly ground black
    pepper

*For the béchamel sauce:*
½ pint (275ml) milk
1 oz (25g) butter
1 tablespoon fine flour
1 bay leaf

1 onion ring
sliver carrot
parsley stalk
salt and pepper

*The beauty of this dish is that it can be prepared the day before and just popped in the oven before serving.*

Soften the garlic and onion in olive oil. Add the courgettes and sauté for a few minutes.

Add the tinned tomatoes, tomato purée, rosemary, sugar and seasoning and cook until the courgettes are soft and the tomato juice is reduced.

Transfer the courgette mixture to four individual dishes.

Make the béchamel sauce by heating the milk gently through in a pan with the salt, pepper, herbs and vegetables. Leave to stand for 15 minutes. In another pan melt the butter and stir in the flour. Allow to cook for a minute or so without browning. Strain the milk and, stirring all the while, pour into the melted butter. Bring to the boil and cook over a low heat for 10 minutes.

Pour the béchamel sauce equally over the four dishes. Sprinkle breadcrumbs and Parmesan over each dish and bake in the oven at 200°C/400°F/gas 6 for 15–20 minutes or until golden brown.

---

# Falafels

*Serves 6*

*Food For Health, London*
*Chef: Abdel Rahman*

1 lb (450g) yellow split peas, soaked in cold water for 24 hours
1 large onion, finely chopped or 1 bunch spring onions, finely chopped
2 cloves garlic, crushed
small bunch parsley or mint, finely chopped

1 egg
salt
cayenne or hot paprika, to taste
½–1 teaspoon ground coriander
½–1 teaspoon ground cumin
oil for deep fat frying

*This is a very versatile Egyptian savoury which can be used as a main course with salads or as an interesting starter to a meal. They can be served hot or cold.*

Drain the peas and put through a mincer using a fine plate.

Add all the other ingredients and mix well, or better still, leave them to mix in an electric mixer on a slow speed for a minute or two. (In Egypt the ingredients are pounded together by hand.) Leave the mixture in a cool place for 1–2 hours.

Take large teaspoonfuls and shape into rounds, the size of a large walnut. Place the rounds on a baking tin so that one side is flattened. Leave for a short time while the oil is heating. When very hot, drop them in and deep fry until they are a rich brown – at least 5 minutes to allow to cook through.

Serve with a small salad or with pitta bread and tahini.

## Diwana Fritters

*Serves 4–6*

*Diwana Bhel-Poori House, London*
*Chef: Mr Patel*

*For the batter:*
6 oz (175g) wholewheat flour
pinch salt
lovat seeds, crushed, to taste

chilli powder to taste
½ pint (275ml) water

8 oz (225g) aubergine, skinned
  and chopped into bite-sized
  pieces
8 oz (225g) button mushrooms, if
  large cut into halves or
  quarters

oil or ghee for deep fat frying

Make the batter, by gradually stirring the water into the flour and salt until it forms a smooth but thick batter. It should coat the back of a spoon easily. Add the lovat seeds and chilli powder. Leave to stand for 30 minutes.

59

Heat up a pan of deep fat.

Put a few of the aubergines and mushrooms in the batter and coat them evenly. Test the heat of the fat by dropping in one fritter – it should rise to the surface and bubble rapidly. Cook a few fritters at a time until they are golden brown, then lift them out and drain on kitchen paper. Keep warm, uncovered, in the oven until all the fritters are cooked.

---

# Good Food Café Hors D'Oeuvres     *Serves 6*

*Good Food Café, Llandrindod Wells*
*Chefs: Heather Williams and Sue Early*

*For the Cucumber Raita:*
1 cucumber, grated or sliced
5 fl. oz (150ml) natural yoghurt
1 teaspoon salt

½ teaspoon cumin or dill
1 small onion, chopped

*For the Potato Raita:*
1½ (675g) potatoes, peeled and
    cooked
5 fl. oz (150ml) natural yoghurt

1 teaspoon salt
½ teaspoon chilli powder
1 teaspoon cumin

*For the Tomatoes and Onions in Lemon Juice:*
2 onions, thinly
    sliced
1 lb (450g) tomatoes, thinly
    sliced
4 tablespoons lemon juice
    (French dressing can be
    substituted)

salt and black pepper
handful parsley, freshly chopped

*For the Celery, Apple and Sesame Seeds:*
½ head celery, thinly sliced
2 rosy apples, thinly sliced
½ tablespoon sesame seeds

2 tablespoons French dressing
handful freshly chopped chives
    or parsley

60

*These hors d'oeuvres are simple to prepare and delicious to eat. Much of their success is in the presentation so serve them in matching bowls or on a single tray.*

To make the Cucumber Raita, sprinkle the grated cucumber with salt and set aside for one hour to drain. Alternate layers of cucumber, sprinkled with a little onion and cumin, with yoghurt.

To make the Potato Raita, chop the potatoes. Mix in the salt, chilli powder and cumin and leave to cool. Once cold mix in the yoghurt.

To make the Tomato and Onion starter, layer the slices of onion and tomato alternately with the lemon juice, parsley and seasoning.

To make the Celery and Apple starter, mix the celery and apple with the dressing and chopped herbs. Place in a serving dish and sprinkle over the sesame seeds.

---

# Lasagne
Serves 4–6

*Siop Y Chwarel (The Quarry Shop), Machynlleth*
*Chef: Ann Lowmass*

8 oz (225g) wholewheat lasagne verdi
few drops oil
2 onions, peeled and chopped
1 clove garlic, peeled and chopped
1 large tin tomatoes (or the equivalent of fresh), chopped
tomato purée to taste (start with 2 tablespoons)
ground black pepper and sea salt
oregano and basil to taste
4–6 oz (125g–175g) cheese, grated

Put the lasagne in a large saucepan, cover with cold water and add a few drops of oil to prevent it from sticking together. Boil for about

20 minutes or until just tender. Test it by throwing a bit against the wall – if it sticks then it's ready!

Fry the onions and garlic in oil until softened but not brown. Add the tomato purée, chopped tomatoes, salt, pepper and herbs. Boil rapidly to reduce excess liquid and thicken.

Strain and rinse the lasagne and divide between individual bowls. Pour the tomato mixture over the top, then sprinkle some grated cheese over each. Place in the oven or under the grill until the cheese is bubbly and hot.

---

# Minted Melon with Avocado

*Serves 4*

*Marno's, Ipswich*
*Chef: Penny McSheehy*

1 large ripe melon
2 large ripe avocados

French dressing
mint leaves to garnish

Cut the melon in half lengthwise and remove the seeds carefully with a spoon, taking care not to damage the flesh.

Divide each half into 6 to 8 smaller boat-shaped pieces – the number will obviously depend on the size of the melon, but the main thing is to have an equal number of slices for each person.

Arrange the melon slices in fan shapes on four individual dishes.

Cut the avocados in half, remove their stones, and using a small baller, scoop out rounds and drop them into a bowl containing a little French dressing. Coat them lightly with the dressing and place a few balls at the base of each fan.

Sprinkle over a little more dressing and garnish with mint leaves.

# Mushroom Vol au Vents

*The Old Bakehouse, Castle Cary*
*Chef: Susan Roxburgh*

1 small onion, chopped
3 oz (75g) good margarine
pinch mixed herbs
4 oz mushrooms, sliced

1 oz (25g) 81% wholemeal flour
½ pint (275ml) milk
salt and black pepper

8 medium sized vol au vent cases

*Puff pastry is very tricky to make from wholemeal flour, so, unless you are feeling brave, buy the cases ready made. The filling makes enough for eight cases. Serve one each as a starter or two for a main course with a jacket potato and a mixed salad.*

Cook the onion and herbs in the margarine. Add the sliced mushrooms and cook for 5 minutes. Add the flour and stir well until the fat is absorbed. Add the milk, stirring all the time until the sauce is smooth. Season.

Meanwhile, cook the pastry cases in the top of a hot oven, 200°C/ 400°F/gas 6 for 12 minutes. When cool, remove lids and pour in the hot mixture and serve.

# Onion Bhajis with Yoghurt Sauce

*Serves 6*

*York Wholefood Restaurant, York*
*Chef: Joan Woolveridge*

8 oz (225g) rice flour
4 oz (125g) wholemeal flour
1 tablespoon turmeric
1 tablespoon methi (fenugreek leaves available from Indian grocers – a little ground fenugreek will do if unavailable)
1 tablespoon mint, freshly chopped

garam masala or chilli powder to taste
1 lb (450g) onions, finely chopped
fat for deep frying – preferably ghee, obtainable from wholefood shops

## For the yoghurt sauce:

1 large carton natural yoghurt
1 small onion, finely chopped
1 tablespoon garam masala

1 teaspoon cinnamon
1 tablespoon mint, finely chopped

Mix all the dry ingredients together with water to make a stiff batter. Add the onions and beat well.

Drop golf ball sized spoonfuls of the mixture into very hot fat and cook until brown and crisp – fat must be hot enough to seal and crisp them quickly. Drain.

The yoghurt sauce is the work of a moment. Just stir together and chill. Serve the sauce along with a green salad and fresh lemon quarters.

# Ratatouille

*Serves 4–6*

*Nuthouse, London*
*Chef: Abraham Nasr and Magdi Aboulnass*

| | |
|---|---|
| 4 carrots | few mushrooms |
| 4 potatoes | few brussels sprouts |
| 4 swedes | pickling spices or coriander' |
| 3 courgettes | salt and black pepper |
| 2 sticks celery | 2 oz (50g) margarine |
| 3 onions, roughly chopped | |

Half-cook the carrots, potatoes, swedes, courgettes and sprouts in boiling water.

Cut all the vegetables into small, equal-sized pieces.

Melt the margarine in a large frying pan. Add the seasoning and then the onion and celery. Sauté for a few minutes and then add the rest of the vegetables. Fry until all the vegetables are just tender, adjust seasoning and serve very hot.

# Spinach Pancakes with a Sherry and Mushroom Sauce

*Serves 4–6*

*Season's Kitchen, Forest Row*
*Chef: Liz Boisseau*

*For the batter:*
4 oz (125g) 85% flour
2 eggs
½ pint (225ml) milk

pinch salt
1 dessertspoon oil

*For the filling:*
good 2 lb (generous kilo) fresh
   spinach
3 oz (75g) cottage cheese
3–4 oz (75g–125g) Cheddar,
   grated
3 eggs

sprinkling nutmeg
salt and black pepper
1 tablespoon béchamel sauce,
   reserved from the topping
   sauce

*For the mushroom sauce:*
1 pint (450ml) milk
   infused with 1 teaspoonful
   peppercorns, parsley stalks,
   1 slice carrot, 1 onion, 2 bay
   leaves, 1 stick celery
1½ oz (40g) flour
1½ oz (40g) margarine or butter

6–8 oz (175g–225g) mushrooms,
   finely sliced, preferably by a
   Magi-mix
salt and pepper
1 good tablespoon sherry
lemon juice (optional)

chopped fresh parsley to garnish

*These pancakes are just as successful if made and filled a day ahead.*

Place the spinach in a steamer and cook for about 20 minutes until tender. Press and drain to remove excess moisture, then chop up finely.

Make the batter by mixing the ingredients together until smooth. Leave to stand for 30 minutes.

Make the béchamel sauce by melting the fat. Stir in the flour, cook slightly and then gradually add the strained milk. Bring to the boil and stir until the sauce is thick and smooth. Flavour with sherry, salt, pepper, nutmeg and lemon juice if desired. Leave the sauce for as long as possible at this stage in an uncovered pan, on a thread of heat, or preferably in a bain marie, to allow it to become really thick and creamy. About half an hour before you need the sauce, add the mushrooms, cover the pan and allow them to cook lightly on a very low heat.

Mix the chopped spinach with the cottage cheese, Cheddar, 3 eggs and 1 tablespoon of the béchamel. Season with salt, pepper and nutmeg. Pour this mixture into a baking dish and bake at 180°C/350°F/gas 4 for about 30 minutes or until set.

Fry the pancakes in a little oil. This quantity will make 12 small ones or 6 large.

Fill the pancakes with the cooked spinach mixture, roll up and place in a casserole dish covered with foil at 180°C/350°F/gas 4. After 10 minutes remove the foil and continue heating until the pancakes are warmed through.

Just before serving, pour the sauce over the top and sprinkle with chopped parsley.

# Stuffed Tomatoes

*Serves 8*

*Stanards, Canterbury*
*Chef: Jacky Luckhurst*

8 medium tomatoes
1 large onion, finely chopped
2 oz (50g) mushrooms, finely
    chopped
4 oz (125g) grated Cheddar or
    cottage cheese

pinch mixed herbs
little fat for frying
8 lettuce leaves to garnish
parsley to garnish

Stand each tomato on its flattest side, where the stalk was, and slice the top off. Scoop out the core and seeds and discard them. Put the tomatoes to one side.

Fry the onions and mushrooms in the fat until tender. Drain and leave to cool.

Mix the onions and mushrooms with the cheese and add the herbs.

Spoon the mixture into the tomato cases and replace the lids. Chill. Serve each tomato on a lettuce leaf garnished with a sprig of parsley.

---

# Tzatziki

*Serves 4*

*Food For Thought, Sherborne*
*Chefs: Michael and Margaret Balfour*

1 large cucumber, grated or
    finely chopped
1 tablespoon chopped fresh mint
    or 1 teaspoon dried

¼ pint (150ml) plain
    unsweetened yoghurt
salt and black pepper

The excellent thing about this dish is the potential it offers for experimentation and variety. Recipes for this dish are to be found in almost every country from the eastern Mediterranean to India. It is diluted with more yoghurt in Lebanon and served as a cold soup. In Cyprus they add onion and call it Talatourie, and in India it is Kakri Raita when chopped coriander leaves and a little chilli can be used instead of mint. There are other examples such as Cacik in Turkey and Tarator in Yugoslavia. Different salad vegetables can be added such as red pepper, but the most popular extra ingredient is a crushed clove of garlic.

Tzatziki itself is a Greek dish and in the summer months customers at our restaurant sit in the courtyard by the hanging baskets and tubs of flowers, eat their tzatziki and dream of holidays in Greece!

Dry the excess moisture off the chopped cucumber by patting with absorbent paper.

Mix the yoghurt and mint with the cucumber and season to taste. Pop a fresh sprig of mint on top to decorate.

---

# Stir-Fried Vegetables in Seasame Orange Sauce

*Serves 6–8*

*Delany's, Shrewsbury*
*Chefs: Odotto and Bolinda*

Selection of vegetables below according to season:

2 onions, chopped
2 large carrots, chopped
2 large leeks, chopped
small cauliflower, chopped

small red cabbage, chopped
red and green pepper, chopped
4 oz (125g) mushrooms, chopped
3 courgettes, chopped

sunflower or soya oil
2 cloves garlic, crushed
good sprinkling tarragon
juice 3 oranges and grated rind of 2 oranges

3 tablespoons tahini
vegetable stock or water
salt and pepper
lemon juice and tamari

In bowl, mix the juice of the oranges with the tahini until the mixture is smooth. Add vegetable stock to make 1 pint (575ml) liquid.

Stir-fry (in a wok if possible) the vegetables in a small amount of sunflower or soya oil until just tender. Put the slower cooking vegetables in first and the quicker ones in later. Add the orange and tahini mixture and rapidly stir-fry until heated through. Season to taste with salt, pepper, lemon juice and tamari.

Serve with brown rice.

---

# Zoomamadooma
*Serves 6*

*Hockneys, Croydon*
*Chef: Steve Webster*

8 oz (225g) red kidney beans,
   pre-soaked
1 onion, sliced
1 clove garlic, crushed
1½ teaspoons basil
¾ teaspoon oregano
¾ teaspoon mixed herbs
1 lb (450g) potatoes, peeled and
   chopped
14 oz (400g) tin tomatoes,
   roughly chopped with their
   juice

1 green pepper
4 oz (125g) button mushrooms,
   halved
salt and black pepper
4 oz (125g) frozen peas
2 tablespoons shoyu/tamari
2 oz (50g) butter
oil for frying

Drain the soaked beans and place in a large saucepan with an equal quantity of water. Place over a medium heat and leave to cook.

Sauté the garlic, onion and herbs in a little oil. When soft add them to the beans. Add the chopped potatoes and tomatoes with their juice.

Sauté the pepper and mushrooms in the butter. Add to the 'Zooma'. Test the beans and if nearly ready season with salt.

About 10 minutes before the end of the cooking time add the peas, shoyu and seasoning to taste. Cook until the peas are ready. Serve with bread and you will find it almost a meal in itself.

# Main Dishes

## Apple and Onion Bake

*Serves 4–6*

*Clinchs Salad House, Chichester*
*Chef: Mrs A. Ellis*

1 lb (450g) potatoes
3 medium onions, thinly sliced
2 oz (50g) butter

1 tablespoon oil
3 cooking apples
salt and black pepper

*For the cheese sauce:*
1 pint (575ml) milk, infused with
   1 bay leaf, mace and
   peppercorns
2 oz (50g) butter

2 oz (50g) flour
1 rounded teaspoon made
   mustard
4 oz (125g) grated cheese

*For the topping:*
2 oz (50g) grated cheese

2 oz (50g) wholemeal breadcrumbs

Scrub the potato skins and slice or cube the potatoes and cook gently in salted water until just cooked.

Sauté the onion in the oil and butter until soft but not coloured. Quarter and core the apples but do not peel them. Cut into thin slices.

Make the cheese sauce by melting the butter and adding the flour. Cook for 2–3 minutes and gradually add the warm milk. Stir until thick, add the grated cheese and mustard, taste and season.

To assemble, grease a 2½ pint (1¼ litre) ovenproof dish. Place half the onions in the bottom of the dish and cover with half of the potatoes followed by half the apples. Season as you go. Pour over half the sauce. Repeat the layers, finishing with the sauce.

Mix the cheese and crumb topping together and sprinkle on top. Bake at 190°C/375°F/gas 5 for about 45 minutes until brown and bubbling. Serve with a bowl of mixed salad.

---

# Stuffed Aubergines

*Serves 4*

*Harvest, London*
*Chef: Giuseppe Rossi*

2 large aubergines, washed
1 onion, finely chopped
1 clove garlic, finely chopped
2 stalks celery, finely sliced
6 oz (175g) mushrooms, finely chopped
1 carrot, finely diced
2 oz (50g) garden peas
2 tomatoes, skinned and roughly chopped

½ red or green pepper, diced
2 oz (50g) cooked brown rice
2 oz (50g) breadcrumbs
1 teaspoon mixed herbs
nutmeg
salt and freshly ground black pepper
2 tablespoons vegetable oil

*For the tomato sauce:*
1 large onion, finely chopped
1 lb (450g) tin tomatoes
1 clove garlic, crushed
2 tablespoons tomato purée
½ pint (275ml) water

1 teaspoon oregano
1 bay leaf
salt and pepper
4 oz (125g) mushrooms, chopped
3 tablespoons vegetable oil

6–8 oz (175–225g) mature Cheddar, grated

Make the tomato sauce by heating the oil in a saucepan. Sauté the onion until soft, then add the mushrooms and sauté gently. Add the garlic, seasoning, tomatoes, tomato purée and water and bring to the boil, stirring from time to time, then simmer for 30 minutes. The sauce should be of a consistency to cover the back of a wooden spoon – if it needs thickening add about a dessertspoon of cornflour to a little sauce and then add it to the pan. Bring back to the boil, stirring well. Add more cornflour if required.

Slice the aubergines lengthways and taking care not to damage the skins, scoop out the flesh. Reserve the skins. Place the flesh in a pan of salted water, cover and boil until tender. Remove and drain.

Put the 2 tablespoons of oil in a large pan and sauté the onion, garlic and aubergine. Add the celery, mushrooms, carrots, peas, tomatoes and pepper and fry together until tender. Season.

Combine the breadcrumbs and rice together in a large bowl and add the fried ingredients and mix well. Season.

Place the aubergine skins in an ovenproof dish and fill each one with stuffing, piling it up quite high. Pour over the tomato sauce and sprinkle the top of each aubergine with the grated cheese.

Place in an oven heated to 180°C/350°F/gas 4 for about 20 minutes until the cheese is bubbling and the aubergines are heated through.

# Brazil Nut Roast En Croûte

Serves 6–8

*Harvest, Ambleside*
*Chef: Gillian Kelly*

6 oz (175g) chick peas
6 oz (175g) Brazil nuts, ground
6 oz (175g) wholemeal
  breadcrumbs
1 large onion, peeled and finely
  chopped
7 oz (175g) mushrooms, finely
  chopped

salt and black pepper
1 dessertspoon yeast extract
1 generous teaspoon mixed herbs
8 oz (225g) shortcrust pastry
  made with 85% wheatmeal
  flour
oil for frying

*This is a marvellous dish for special occasions – ideal for Christmas dinner – served with roast potatoes, brussels sprouts, roast parsnips and apple sauce. You can also serve it with a savoury mushroom sauce or tomato sauce.*

Soak the chick peas overnight. Change the water and cook in salted boiling water for 1 hour or until tender.

Blend together the chick peas and yeast extract.

Mix together the ground Brazil nuts and breadcrumbs and then stir in the chick peas.

Sauté the onion and mushrooms together gently in a little oil until they form their own liquid. Add them to the nut and breadcrumb mixture.

Add salt and black pepper and herbs to taste. Mix thoroughly.

Line a 2 lb (generous litre) loaf tin with the pastry, reserving enough pastry to make a lid. Bake blind at 200°C/400°F/gas 6 for about 10 minutes.

Fill the pastry case with the nut roast mixture and bake for 15 minutes. Then turn the heat down to 160°C/300°F/gas 2 for 15 minutes more. Turn out of the loaf tin and slice.

---

# Cheese Soufflé

*Food For Health, London*
*Chef: John Cross*

*Serves 4*

2 oz (50g) butter
about 2 oz (50g) 81% wheatmeal
   flour
½ pint (275ml) milk
6 egg yolks and 8 egg whites or 6
   large separated eggs or 8
   medium separated eggs

salt and pepper
4–6 oz (125–175g) grated
   Cheddar cheese

Butter a heatproof dish and heat the oven to 200°C/400°F/gas 6.

Melt the butter and stir in enough flour to make a roux. Add the milk and cook until a really thick sauce is formed.

Draw away from the heat and beat in the cheese and then the egg yolks. The mixture is now of a slacker consistency and it is easier to fold in the stiffly beaten egg whites. These can be beaten in a mixer with the seasoning while the rest of the soufflé is being made or whip them just before you start if beating by hand.

Pour the mixture into the dish and bake for 25–30 minutes – the time will depend on the depth of the baking dish. If the top is becoming very brown, reduce the heat for the last minutes. Serve as soon as possible.

Below are listed some variations for you to try:

(1) Vary the type of cheese e.g. Parmesan, Gruyère, Sage Derby.

(2) Add cooked mushrooms 4–8 oz (125–225g) to the yolk and cheese mixture before folding in the whites.

(3) Place some parboiled cauliflower in the bottom of the baking dish and pour the soufflé mixture over the top.

(4) Add chopped spring onion, chives, parsley, mint, watercress to the mixture just before baking. Experiment with different combinations and amounts.

(5) Add lightly cooked but dry pieces of other cooked vegetables either stirred into the mixture at the bottom of the dish or layered in the soufflé mixture for a surprise. Examples might be aubergines, green peppers, tomatoes or sweetcorn.

*First published by Faber in 'The Home Book of Vegetarian Cookery' by N. B. and R. Highton*

---

# Layered Millet and Mushroom Pancakes   *Serves 4–6*

*York Wholefood Restaurant, York*
*Chef: Gillian Hull*

*For the millet mixture:*

8 oz (225g) millet
2 oz (50g) Brazil nuts, broken up
10 oz (275g) tin tomatoes
1 tablespoon tomato purée
1 large onion, chopped
1 green pepper, roughly chopped

1 large carrot, roughly chopped
2 cloves garlic, crushed
fresh parsley
1–2 teaspoons oregano
salt and pepper
oil/fat

*For the batter*

2 eggs
6 oz (175g) wholemeal flour

¾–1 pint (425ml–575ml) milk
pinch salt

For the mushroom sauce:

6 oz (175g) mushrooms, roughly chopped
oil/fat
½ pint (275ml) milk
½ pint (275ml) water

2 oz (50g) rice flour
1 teaspoon fresh dill or basil or ½ teaspoon if dried
shoyu/soya sauce to taste
pepper

For the topping:

½ cup brown breadcrumbs

2 oz (50g) grated cheese

*Don't make the mistake of thinking of millet as being only fit for budgies! The tiny golden grains are highly nutritious and form a basic part of the diet of the peoples of Africa and Asia. Millet swells considerably when cooked and needs at least three times its dry volume in water. It takes about 30 minutes to cook. Millet flakes can be cooked like porridge oats for breakfast or used in puddings (sweet and savoury) or soups and stews. This delicious dish requires some work on your part but the results make it all worthwhile.*

Make the batter by beating the eggs into the flour and salt. Then gradually blend in the milk until the batter pours but is not too thin.

Sauté the millet with the onion in some oil or fat until the onion is clear and tender, then cook together in three times the volume of water for about 30 minutes.

Sauté the pepper, garlic and carrot in oil until tender. Add to the millet mixture along with the nuts, tomatoes and purée. Add chopped parsley, oregano and seasoning. Simmer until pancakes and sauce are ready, adding water if the mixture gets too thick.

Beat the batter again and add a little extra milk if necessary. Cook the pancakes – the quantity of batter should give you about 6–8. As you cook the pancakes pile them up interleaved with greaseproof paper.

Cook the mushrooms along with the dill in a little oil, add the water and milk and simmer. Blend the rice flour with cold water to make a thin paste, then pour into the hot milk, stirring all the time and bring to the boil. Season with shoyu/soya sauce and pepper and cook for few minutes.

Grease an ovenproof dish of a suitable size and put a layer of pancake at the bottom and then build up alternate layers of millet mixture, pancake and sauce finishing with a layer of pancake. Sprinkle the top with cheese and breadcrumbs and bake at 170°C/325°F/gas 3 for 30 minutes or until the topping is crisp and brown.

Serve with a steamed green vegetable.

---

# Moussaka

*Serves 6*

*Harvest, London*
*Chef: Giuseppe Rossi*

1 lb (450g) potatoes, peeled and
   thinly sliced
1½ lb (675g) aubergines
2 courgettes, chopped into ½"
   rings

1 pepper, cut into strips
vegetable oil
grated Parmesan cheese

*For the cheese sauce:*
1 oz (25g) margarine
2 tablespoons 81% wheatmeal
   flour
1 pint (575ml) milk
generous sprinkling black
   pepper

½ teaspoon nutmeg
pinch fresh or dried herbs
4 oz (125g) mature Cheddar,
   grated
1 bay leaf

*For the tomato sauce:*
1 large onion, finely chopped
14 oz (400g) tin tomatoes
1 clove garlic, crushed
2 tablespoons tomato purée
½ pint (275ml) water

½ pint oregano
1 bay leaf
salt and black pepper
4 oz (125g) mushrooms, chopped
3 tablespoons vegetable oil

Slice the aubergines thinly, sprinkle with salt and put to one side for about 20 minutes.

Make the cheese sauce by putting the milk in a saucepan. Add the bay leaf, nutmeg, herbs and bring to the boil. Take off the heat and leave the flavours to infuse. Melt the margarine in another pan and add the flour and cook until it bubbles. Strain the milk and add it gradually to the roux, stirring all the time. Cook for about 5 minutes to allow the sauce to thicken and for the flour granules to burst. Add the cheese and cook just enough for the cheese to melt without going stringy. Check the seasoning and put to one side.

Make the tomato sauce by heating the oil in a pan. Sauté the onions until soft, then add the mushrooms and sauté gently. Add the garlic and seasoning and then the tomatoes, water and tomato purée. Bring to the boil, stirring from time to time. Cover the pan and simmer for about 30 minutes. The sauce should be thick enough to coat the back of a spoon. If necessary, thicken the sauce with a little cornflour. Adjust seasoning and put to one side.

Heat 2–3 tablespoons of oil in a large pan and fry the sliced aubergines until soft but firm. Drain and keep warm. Fry the potatoes until just tender and then fry the courgettes and pepper until just soft.

Take an ovenproof dish. Cover the bottom with a layer of cheese and then the tomato sauce. Place the aubergines, courgettes, pepper and potatoes on top in layers. Sprinkle with Parmesan. Cover with another layer of cheese sauce and then tomato sauce, making sure all the vegetables are covered. Repeat this process until all the vegetables are used. Finally, cover with a layer of sauce, sprinkle with grated cheese and place in the oven at 180°C/350°F/gas 4 for about 20 minutes until the dish is heated through and the cheese is golden on top.

# Nuthouse Nut Rissoles

*Serves 4–6*

*Nuthouse, London*
*Chefs: Abraham Nasr and Magdi Aboulnass*

4 oz (125g) mixed nuts, chopped
   or grated
8 oz (225g) breadcrumbs
3 pre-cooked carrots, grated
1 large pre-cooked potato, grated
2 medium sized apples, cored
   and grated

1 teaspoon mixed herbs
1 teaspoon mixed spices
1 teaspoon curry powder
water to mix
fat for deep drying

Mixed all the grated ingredients together and add just enough water to bind them together.

Shape into balls or pyramids – this quantity should make about 15–20 rissoles.

Heat the oil to 250°C/500°F – if the oil is not hot enough the rissoles may fall apart during cooking, so take care. Deep fry a few at a time until they are golden brown, drain and keep warm until all the rissoles have been cooked. Serve hot.

# Parmigiana

*Season's Kitchen, Forest Row*
*Chef: Liz Boisseau*

### For the tomato sauce:

1 medium Spanish onion, finely chopped
1 small carrot, finely chopped
1 stem celery, finely chopped
2 cloves garlic, crushed
2 tablespoons vegetable oil – or 1 tablespoon vegetable and 1 tablespoon olive oil
2 big pinches basil
2 big pinches marjoram or oregano
1 pinch sugar
3 × 14 oz (400g) tins tomatoes with juice
1 good dessertspoon tomato purée
salt and pepper to taste

### For the béchamel sauce:

1 pint (450ml) milk infused with 1 spoonful peppercorns, parsley stalks, 1 slice carrot, 1 onion, 2 bay leaves, 1 stick celery
2 oz (50g) flour
2 oz (50g) margarine or butter
salt and pepper

### For the vegetable nut balls:

1 tablespoon onion, finely chopped
1 clove garlic, finely chopped
1 tablespoon finely chopped green pepper or red or mixed
1 tablespoon grated carrot
1 oz (25g) breadcrumbs
1 tablespoon parsley, chopped
2 oz (50g) roasted and ground mixed nuts
small pinch marjoram
salt and pepper
good pinch paprika
1 egg
3 large aubergines
2 hard boiled eggs, finely chopped
4 oz (125g) havarti cheese, cubed
oil for frying
Parmesan cheese
2 oz (50g) butter
1 egg

Make the tomato sauce by softening the onion, garlic, carrot and celery in the oil in a large, heavy bottomed pan. Add the basil, marjoram or oregano and sugar with the tomatoes, purée and seasoning. Simmer, uncovered on a low heat, for at least 1 hour to obtain a rich, full and thick sauce.

For the béchamel sauce, make sure that the milk has been infused with the vegetables for a reasonable length of time. Then make the béchamel in the usual way by melting the fat. Stir in the flour, cook slightly and then add the strained milk, whisking. Bring to the boil and stir until the sauce is thick and smooth. Season and then leave on a thread of heat or in a bain marie for as long as possible to give a thick, beautifully creamy consistency.

Slice the aubergines thinly, lengthwise. Salt them and leave them to drain for an hour in a colander with a weight on top to squeeze out the excess moisture.

Make the vegetable nut balls by binding all the ingredients together with an egg, adding a few more breadcrumbs if the mixture is slack. Shape into balls about the size of a shelled walnut and fry in about ¼" (0.5cm) hot oil until nicely browned. Drain and reserve.

Dry the aubergines off and fry in ½" (1cm) hot oil until they are browned on both sides. Drain and put to one side.

Take about a 2 pint (generous litre) casserole dish and layer the ingredients in the following order:
- (a) on the base, a layer tomato sauce
- (b) a single layer aubergines
- (c) the chopped egg and cubed havarti
- (d) a layer of béchamel sauce, which should be thick enough to spoon on in blobs
- (e) thin layer tomato sauce
- (f) layer of aubergine
- (g) layer of nut balls
- (h) layer of béchamel sauce
- (i) layer of tomato sauce

(j)   layer of aubergine

(k)   beat the remaining béchamel up with an egg and spread over
       the top

(l)   sprinkle the top with Parmesan and dot with butter

Cover the dish and bake for 45 minutes at 180°C/350°F/gas 4.

---

# Pan Fried Noodles with Seitan

*Natural Snack, London*
*Chef: Bretta Carthey*

*For the seitan:*
7 cups of 81% or 85% wheatflour, or a mixture of 100% wholewheat
   flour and unbleached white flour
2½ cups water, approximately

small piece Kombu sea vegetable
shoyu/soya sauce to taste
1 packet noodles, either
   buckwheat (Soba) or wheat
   (Udon)
1 cup onions, thinly sliced

1 cup carrots, cut into
   matchsticks
sesame seeds
spring onions, sliced
oil for frying
2 bunches watercress, washed
   well

*Seitan is wheat gluten, a good quality protein which is very nutritious and easy to digest. It is simply prepared by making a dough from wheat flour and washing out the starch, a bran, leaving a sticky elastic mass of gluten. Save the starch water produced when making the seitan. The starch will settle at the bottom leaving a clear liquid on top. Use the starch for thickening gravies, making creamed soups, thickening stews, making desserts etc. The clear water is wonderful for the complexion, for bathing the hands and face.*

Make the seitan by adding the flour to the water to form a soft dough.

Knead vigorously for 5–10 minutes until the dough is very soft and elastic to the touch – it should feel like one's ear lobe. Leave in a bowl with enough water to cover for at least 10 minutes – it must not be a plastic bowl.

Knead the dough under the soaking water until the water turns milky. Change the water and knead again. Continue kneading the dough in successive changes of water until all the starch and bran are rinsed off and the water remains clear. Squeeze the wheat gluten into one lump and then cut it into bite-sized pieces.

Place the seitan on the Kombu sea vegetable and cover with water. Bring to the boil, then simmer for 30–45 minutes.

Add shoyu to taste and then simmer for 5–10 minutes longer.

Cook the noodles according to the instructions on the packet. Rinse in cold water and allow to dry in a colander. If they are not dry they will stick to the pan when fried.

Lightly cook the onions and carrots in a small amount of boiling water.

Toast the sesame seeds in a pan without oil, stirring constantly.

Fry the seitan in a little oil. Set aside and keep warm.

Clean and oil the pan, put over a high heat and when hot place the noodles in and stir gently with chopsticks for a few moments. Add the vegetables and continue stirring until hot.

Remove from the heat, arrange on a plate, placing the pieces of seitan on top. Garnish with sesame seeds, spring onion and watercress.

# Stuffed Peppers with Mushroom Sauce    *Serves 4*

*Henderson's Salad Table, Edinburgh*
*Chef: Janet Henderson*

6 oz (175g) Brazil nuts, finely
    chopped
4 oz (125g) carrots, washed and
    grated
4 oz (125g) courgettes, washed
    and grated
thyme, to taste

2 oz (50g) butter or oil
2 oz (50g) wholewheat
    breadcrumbs
¼ pint (150ml) vegetable stock
1 egg
4 large peppers
salt and black pepper

*For the mushroom sauce:*
3 oz (75g) butter
2 oz (50g) flour
1 pint (575ml) milk
4 oz (125g) mushrooms, finely
    chopped

salt and black pepper
bay leaf
black mace

Heat the milk with the seasoning and flavourings and bring to the boil. Put to one side and leave to cool for 1 hour. Strain.

Melt the butter gently and cook the nuts and vegetables with the thyme for 5 minutes.

Add the crumbs and vegetable stock to give a moist but firm mixture.

Remove from the heat and add the egg.

Slice the tops off the peppers and remove the seeds. Fill with the stuffing mixture and replace the tops. Put into an ovenproof dish, cover and bake for 30 minutes in a medium oven.

To make the sauce, melt the butter and add the mushrooms. Fry until soft and then stir in the flour and cook for another 2 minutes. Remove from the heat and gradually stir in the strained milk. Return to the heat and bring to the boil, stirring all the time.

Serve the peppers hot, accompanied by the sauce. Delicious.

---

# Wholewheat Pizza

*Serves 6*

*Neal's Yard Bakery, London*
*Chef: Rachel Haigh*

*For the dough:*
1 oz (25g) fresh yeast
½ pint (275ml) warm water
21 oz (600g) wholewheat flour
½ teaspoon salt

*For the sauce:*
14 oz (400g) tin tomatoes
1 tablespoon tomato purée
1 teaspoon oregano
2 cloves garlic (more if desired)
salt and black pepper
pinch chilli powder

*For the topping:*
2–3 tomatoes, sliced into rings
mushrooms, chopped (quantity to preference)
green pepper, chopped (quantity to preference)
onion, chopped (quantity to preference)
few olives and tomato rings to decorate
9 oz (250g) cheese, grated

You can make a vegan pizza by substituting 9 oz (250g) tofu for the cheese.

Crumble the yeast into the warm water and stir in 12 oz (350g) of the flour to make a thick batter. Cover and leave in a warm place to rise for about 30 minutes.

Add the ½ teaspoon salt and work in the remaining flour until the dough holds together. Turn onto a lightly oiled surface and knead. The dough should be strong and elastic and not stick to your hands. Return to the bowl when smooth and leave to rise for another 30 minutes.

Punch down, divide into two and roll out onto a floured board. Oil two trays of about 12″×8″ (30cm×20cm) and line with the dough, pushing it up the sides. Put the ingredients for the sauce into a blender and mix thoroughly. Spread the sauce over the dough.

Sprinkle over the chopped vegetables. Cover with the cheese and decorate with olives and tomato rings. Sprinkle over some more herbs if desired. Bake for about 15 minutes at 250°C/500°F/gas 10.

---

# Pan Haggarty

*Serves 4*

*Super Natural, Newcastle upon Tyne*
*Chef: James Leitch*

6 large potatoes
1 large onion, peeled and finely
   sliced
6 oz (175g) Cheddar cheese,
   grated

vegetable stock or water
seasoning
parsley, freshly chopped to
   garnish

*This very simple recipe is our version of a traditional Northumbrian dish. Many years ago these ingredients would be cooked in a frying pan on top of the coal fired kitchen range.*

Scrub the potatoes and boil them in their jackets until three-parts cooked. When cool, prise off their skins and cut them into ¼″ slices.

Place the onions, grated cheese and potato slices in a deep casserole in layers, seasoning each layer.

Half fill the casserole with the stock.

Cook at 180°C/350°F/gas 4 for about 30 minutes or until the top is golden brown.

Just before serving, sprinkle over the chopped parsley. Delicious served with a watercress and mushroom salad.

---

## Potatoes Romanoff
*Serves 6*

*Grapevine, Birmingham*
*Chef: Mrs Pat Gully*

4½ lb (2kg) potatoes
8 oz (225g) carton live natural
   yoghurt
5 cloves garlic, crushed
8 oz (225g) cottage cheese

salt and freshly ground black
   pepper
3–4 fresh tomatoes, sliced
1–2 oz (25–50g) Cheddar, grated

Scrub and boil the potatoes. Drain and mash with the yoghurt.

Add the garlic, cottage cheese and seasoning and mix together well.

Place in an ovenproof dish and cover the top with the sliced tomatoes. Cover in tin foil and bake at 220°C/425°F/gas 7 for 30–40 minutes.

Remove from the oven, sprinkle with grated cheese and just before serving brown under the grill.

# Ratatouille Quiche

*Serves 4*

*Food For Thought, Sherborne*
*Chefs: Michael and Margaret Balfour*

*For the pastry:*

| | |
|---|---|
| 8 oz (225g) 100% wholewheat flour | 1 egg |
| 4 oz (125g) butter | water to mix |

*A selection of the following vegetables:*

| | |
|---|---|
| onions | courgettes |
| tomatoes | mushrooms |
| green pepper | pre-cooked aubergine |

| | |
|---|---|
| 1 egg | 4 oz (125g) Cheddar cheese, |
| ¼ pint (150ml) milk | grated |

*This is a very versatile and adaptable quiche which can be served cold or hot and can be reheated.*

To make the pastry, rub the butter into the flour until it resembles fine breadcrumbs. Mix in the beaten egg and sufficient water to make the dough pliable for easy rolling. Roll out to fit a well-greased 8" (20cm) flan tin – a loose bottomed tin will make it easier to remove. Bake blind in an oven pre-heated to 190°C/375°F/gas 4 for 10 minutes, and for a further 10 minutes without the baking beans to dry the pastry out.

Spread the grated cheese over the pastry case and cover evenly with the chopped vegetables. Mix the egg and milk together and pour over. Lower the oven temperature to 180°C/350°F/gas 4 and cook for about 30 minutes until the custard is set and the top is just starting to brown.

# Tropical Risotto

*Grapevine, Birmingham*
*Chef: Pat Gully*

12 oz (350g) brown rice
3 or 4 large cooking onions,
 chopped
4 cloves garlic, crushed
about 2″ length fresh ginger,
 chopped
1 teaspoon sea salt
1 eating apple, chopped
3 courgettes, chopped into rings
1 red pepper, chopped

3 or 4 tomatoes
1 tablespoon currants
1 banana, sliced
½ fresh pineapple, cut into cubes
1 tablespoon tomato purée
tamari
sunflower oil
yoghurt to garnish
sliced banana or egg to garnish

Pressure cook the brown rice for 14 minutes. Drain and rinse well in cold water.

In a saucepan sauté the onions, garlic, ginger, apple, courgettes, red pepper, tomatoes, currants and salt in the oil.

When soft add the banana, pineapple and tomato purée

Add the rice and tamari and stir. Allow the rice to heat through and add a drop of water if the mixture is too dry.

Serve in bowls topped with yoghurt, sliced banana or egg.

# Spinach and Cream Cheese Nut Crumble     *Serves 6*

*Delany's, Shrewsbury*
*Chefs: Belinda and Odette*

3 lb (1.5kg) fresh spinach, washed
2 medium onions, chopped
2 medium cloves garlic, crushed
8 oz (225g) cream cheese
1 teaspoon tarragon
1 teaspoon nutmeg
4 oz (125g) ground peanuts

2 oz (50g) wholewheat breadcrumbs
2 oz (50g) rolled oats
2 oz (50g) wholewheat flour
1 dessertspoon tamari
lemon juice
salt and black pepper
sunflower oil

Put the spinach, onions, garlic and tarragon into a pan with a little oil. Cover and steam until just tender. Season with salt and black pepper, lemon juice and nutmeg. Stir in the cheese and pour into a shallow dish.

Make the crumble by mixing the peanuts, breadcrumbs, oats and flour. Add tamari to taste and oil to moisten. The mixture should just hold together if squeezed in your hand.

Sprinkle the crumble over the spinach and bake at 180°C/350°F/gas 4 for about 30 minutes or until lightly browned.

This dish is absolutely delicious served with a potato gratin and a tossed green salad.

# Spinach, Mushrooms and Whole Rice with Cheese Sauce

*Nettles, Cambridge*
*Chef: Mary Ann Marks*

8 oz (225g) mushrooms
2 fl. oz (50ml) shoyu
2 lb (900g) spinach, cooked
½ cup grated cheese
salt and pepper

1 lb (450g) whole brown rice, boiled
vegetable oil for frying
1 onion chopped

*For the cheese sauce:*
¼ cup oil
¼ cup wholemeal flour
salt and pepper
pinch nutmeg

1 pint (575ml) mixed milk and water
1 teaspoon mustard
4–5 oz (125–150g) cheese, grated

2 oz (50g) cheese, grated

Fry the mushrooms in a little oil until tender.

Mix with the shoyu, spinach, grated cheese and seasoning.

Fry the onion and mix with the boiled rice.

To make the cheese sauce, stir the flour, salt and pepper, nutmeg and mustard into the heated oil and gradually add the milk and water. Bring to the boil and stir in the grated cheese.

Layer a dish with the rice mixture at the bottom, then the spinach mixture, the cheese sauce and finally sprinkle over the 2 oz (50g) grated cheese. Bake at 190°C/375°F/gas 5 for about 30 minutes until the cheese is golden.

# Spinach Tortilla

*Harvest, London*
*Chef: Giuseppe Rossi*

2 lb (1kg) fresh spinach or 1 lb
  (450g) frozen
1 lb (450g) mature Cheddar or
  Edam, grated
4 eggs
2 oz (50g) haricot beans, cooked

1 carrot, grated
1 onion, finely chopped
1 clove garlic, crushed
2 oz (50g) breadcrumbs
little milk
salt and black pepper

Prepare spinach and cook in a little water until tender, drain and chop up roughly.

Mix the beans, carrot, onion, garlic, breadcrumbs and spinach together. Add the eggs and enough mik to make a 'loose' mixture. Season well.

Place in a large, greased baking dish and sprinkle the cheese over the top. Bake at 180°C/350°F/gas 4 for 40 minutes until golden brown and bubbling.

# Savoury Vegetable Crumble

Serves 6

*Mother Nature, Stroud*
*Chef: Cindy*

3 oz (75g) margarine or 3
  tablespoons oil
1 medium onion, chopped
1 potato, peeled and diced
1 carrot, sliced
1 small tin sweetcorn, drained
¼ Chinese cabbage or ¼ white
  cabbage, chopped
4 oz (125g) mushrooms, sliced

1 small swede or 2 parsnips,
  diced
2 tablespoons tamari
1 teaspoon mixed herbs
1 teaspoon chilli sauce
2 tablespoons tomato purée
freshly ground salt and black
  pepper

*For the topping:*
4 oz (125g) wholewheat flour
2 oz (50g) rolled oats
3 oz (75g) margarine

4 oz (125g) grated cheese
1 teaspoon mixed herbs
salt and pepper or paprika

*If you thought that crumbles were only sweet – think again! This crunchy topping makes a perfect foil for the savoury filling.*

Sauté the vegetables in the margarine until they are sizzling. Add the tamari, herbs, chilli sauce, tomato purée and seasoning. Then add about ½ pint (275ml) water to make a sauce, adding a little more water if necessary.

Cook for a few minutes until all the vegetables are tender and the flavours are blended.

To make the topping, mix the flour and oats together, rub in the margarine and then stir in the cheese and seasoning. You should end up with a crumb-like consistency.

Put the vegetable mixture into a suitably sized casserole dish. Sprinkle over the topping and bake in the oven at 180°C/350°F/gas 4 for 35–40 minutes or until the mixture is bubbling and the crumble is browning.

# Siriporn's Scalloped Vegetables

*Food For Thought, London*
*Chef: Siriporn Duncan*

1 large onion, coarsely chopped
1 white (Dutch) cabbage, cut
   into bite-sized pieces
6 sticks celery, thinly sliced
2 tablespoons sunflower oil
5 oz (150g) sweetcorn
1¼ pints (725ml) milk

1 tablespoon cornflour
1 teaspoon ground ginger
12 oz (350g) mushrooms, sliced
1 clove garlic, crushed
salt and freshly ground black
   pepper

*For the topping:*
2 tablespoons sunflower oil
12 oz (350g) fresh wholewheat
   breadcrumbs

8 oz (225g) Cheddar, grated

Heat the oil in a heavy saucepan and sauté the onion and garlic until golden. Add the cabbage and celery and continue to sauté gently until just tender – the vegetables should still retain their crispness.

Add the sweetcorn and enough milk to the vegetables to moisten well. Mix the cornflour with the remaining milk and add to this one or two tablespoons of the warmed milk from the pan. Stir to a smooth paste and pour back into the pan, stirring continuously but gently until the mixture thickens and comes to the boil. Continue stirring, add the ginger and the chopped mushrooms. Season with salt and pepper and pour the mixture into an ovenproof dish.

Prepare the topping by heating the oil in a skillet and adding the breadcrumbs, stirring continuously until nicely browned. Turn onto a plate and when cooled mix in the grated cheese. Sprinkle onto the pie and bake in a moderate oven for 15–20 minutes.

# Stanards Special

*Serves 4–6*

*Stanards, Canterbury*
*Chef: Jacky Luckhurst*

2 oz (50g) peas
3 parsnips, chopped
6 carrots, sliced
2 oz (50g) sweetcorn
4 oz (125g) beansprouts
2 oz (50g) cashew nuts
1 oz (25g) peanuts or hazelnuts
2 large pinches mixed herbs
4 oz (125g) vegetable margarine

4 oz (125g) 100% wholemeal
  flour
1 pint (575ml) milk
6 fl. oz (175ml) white wine
8 oz (225g) grated cheese
  (optional)
½ oz (25g) sunflower seeds
parsley, freshly chopped

Cook the parsnips and carrots in separate pans of salted boiling water until tender.

Lightly oil a large baking dish or casserole. Put the beansprouts and nuts on the bottom, followed by the sweetcorn, peas, parsnips and carrots and then a sprinkling of mixed herbs.

Make a wholemeal sauce by melting the margarine in a saucepan. Stir in the flour and cook slightly, then slowly add the milk, stirring constantly. Add a pinch of mixed herbs, check seasoning and cook until the sauce boils and thickens. Take off the heat and stir in the wine.

Pour the sauce all over the vegetables in the casserole. Sprinkle the sunflower seeds (and cheese if wanted) over the top. Place in the oven pre-heated to 200°C/400°F/gas 6 for about 30 minutes until the top is browning.

Just before serving sprinkle over the chopped parsley.

# Marianne's Tagliatelle

*Marno's, Ipswich*
*Chef: Marianne Lungley*

1 large onion, finely sliced
8 oz (225g) mushrooms, sliced
1 clove garlic, crushed
1 dessertspoon wholemeal flour
5 fl. oz (150ml) white wine
5 fl. oz (150ml) whipping cream
½ pint (275ml) milk

8 oz (225g) wholemeal pasta,
  tagliatelle or shell shaped
2 oz (50g) cheese, grated
oil for frying

Fry the onion in a little oil until transparent. Add the mushroom and garlic and cook until soft.

Stir in the flour, add the wine and allow to amalgamate slightly before adding the cream. Stir thoroughly while pouring on the milk and allow to simmer very gently for a few minutes.

While the sauce is simmering, cook the pasta as directed on the packet until just tender.

Drain and then add to the sauce. Remove the pan from the heat, making sure that the pasta is well mixed with the sauce, and pour into a greased casserole. Top with the cheese and bake in a moderate oven, 180°C/350°F/gas 4 for 20 minutes.

# Tofu and Ginger Stir-Fried Vegetables    *Serves 3–4*

*Huckleberry's, Bath*
*Chef: Maggie Walter*

¼" (.6cm) root ginger, minced
8 oz (225g) tofu, diced into ¼"
   (.6cm) cubes
½ cup soya sayce/shoyu
oil
1 clove garlic, crushed
1 cup onion, chopped
1 cup carrots, cut into julienne
   strips

½ cup celery, chopped
2 cups any other vegetables, as
   desired (mushrooms,
   courgette etc.)
½ cup green pepper, chopped
1 cup tinned tomatoes and juice
   seasoned with celery salt
parsley or mustard cress to
   garnish

Soak the tofu pieces in the shoyu for at least 30 minutes.

On a medium heat, cook the ginger and garlic for 2–3 minutes in the oil, stirring all the time.

Add the onions and carrots. Cover and allow to sweat for 2–3 minutes.

Add the celery and mixed vegetables. Then add the green pepper and tofu with shoyu and stir.

Add the tomato mixture, bring to the boil and simmer for a minute, stirring all the time.

Serve immediately on a bed of rice or bulgar. Garnish with parsley or mustard cress.

# Vegetable Cheese Cobbler

*Serves 6*

*Nature's Way, Eastbourne*
*Chefs: Maurice and Dorothy Fossit*

1½ oz (40g) butter beans, cooked
8 oz (225g) onions, sliced
4 oz (125g) potatoes, cooked and
 sliced thinly
2 sticks celery, cooked and cut
 into 1" slices
2 oz (50g) parsnips, sliced and
 cooked

8 oz (225g) tomatoes, skinned
 and quartered
¾ pint (425ml) stock
salt and black pepper
4 oz (125g) green beans

*For the cobbler topping:*
8 oz (225g) 85% plain flour
4 rounded teaspoons baking
 powder
pinch pepper

2 oz (50g) margarine
5 oz (150g) Cheddar cheese,
 grated
milk to mix

*This is an absolutely delicious way to use up any leftover vegetables.*

Cook the onions in a little margarine until soft but not coloured.

Layer all the vegetables in an ovenproof dish in the order given in the list of ingredients. Season.

Add the vegetable stock to cover and place a lid on. Place into the oven at 200°C/400°F/gas 6 for about 45 minutes, until bubbling hot.

To make the cobbler topping, rub the margarine into the flour. Add the pepper, baking powder, 4 oz (125g) of the cheese and mix to a soft dough with the milk. Roll ¾"(2cm) thick and cut into rounds. Arrange over the vegetables, brush with milk and sprinkle over the remaining cheese. Bake uncovered for about 20 minutes until golden brown.

# Vegetable Pancakes with Hazelnut Sauce  *Serves 4–6*

*Gannets, Newark*
*Chef: Hilary Bower*

### For the pancakes:
6 oz (175g) 85% wholemeal flour
2 eggs
¾ pint (425ml) milk

1 tablespoon vegetable oil
pinch salt
oil to fry

### For the filling:
3 carrots, diced
2 sticks celery, diced
2 medium onions, diced
1 leek, diced
1 medium potato, diced

(any other suitable seasonal
  vegetable may be substituted)
salt and pepper
1 oz (25g) butter

### For the sauce:
2–3 fl. oz (50–75ml) single cream
4 oz (125g) 85% plain wholemeal
  flour
4 oz (125g) butter
scant 2 pints (1 litre) cooking
  stock reserved from vegetables

4 oz (125g) ground hazelnuts
4 oz (125g) button mushrooms,
  roughly chopped

*If blessed with a multitude of kitchen utensils it is preferable to cook the pancakes in individual dishes as it may be difficult to serve them when cooked altogether in one large dish.*

To make the pancakes, whisk all the ingredients together using half the milk. Beat well until smooth and creamy and gradually add the remaining milk. Leave to stand for about 30 minutes. This quantity will make approximately 8 pancakes using an 8″ pan. They can be made well in advance and stacked, interleaved with greaseproof paper.

To make the filling, fry all the diced vegetables in the butter for just a few minutes. Add seasoning and some water just to cover. Bring to the boil and simmer until almost cooked. Drain, reserving the cooking juices which should be made up to 2 pints (1 litre) using milk.

Make the sauce by melting the butter in a saucepan. Add the mushrooms and sauté for a few minutes. Add the flour, stir and continue to cook for 2–3 minutes. Gradually add the stock mixture, stirring continuously. Bring to the boil and allow to cool for a while before adding the cream and 3 oz (75g) hazelnuts. Check seasoning.

Pour about 1 pint (575ml) of sauce over the vegetables and stir until evenly coated. Divide this mixture carefully between pancakes and roll up securely. Place in an ovenproof dish with the joins facing downwards.

Coat the pancakes with the remaining sauce and sprinkle with hazelnuts. Bake at 200°C/400°F/gas 6 for 30–35 minutes until bubbling and browning.

---

# Vegetable Strogonoff                     *Serves 4–6*

*Hockneys, Croydon*
*Chef: Ian Flitman*

3 large carrots, diced
2 medium potatoes, diced
½ cauliflower or 12 oz (350g)
   broccoli
1½ lb (674g) mushrooms
1 small onion, sliced
1 pepper, sliced
3 large courgettes, sliced
3 oz (75g) butter
2 tablespoons wholewheat flour
6 oz (150g) sour cream

4 oz (125g) natural yoghurt
7 fl. oz (200ml) Italian red wine
2 teaspoons dill
1½ teaspoons paprika
shoyu/tamari to taste
4 oz (125g) whole wheat
   tagliatelle
milk, as necessary
tomato slices to garnish
salt and black pepper

Cook the carrots, potatoes and cauliflower in a little water until tender. Drain and put to one side.

In the butter, sauté the onion, courgettes, pepper and mushrooms. Add the flour and cook slightly. Mix in the yoghurt, wine and sour cream with the dill, paprika, shoyu and salt and black pepper to taste. Cook gently and add a little mik if the sauce is too thick – it should pour slowly. (You will find that this sauce can easily be modified into an excellent soup!)

Cook the tagliatelle in boiling salted water with a little oil and drain.

In an oiled dish, layer the tagliatelle, then the vegetables and lastly the sauce. Place in the oven at 190°C/375°F/gas 5 for 15 minutes or until heated through. Garnish with tomato slices and serve.

---

# Wholewheat Fricassée

*Serves 4*

*Cranks, London*

8 oz (225g) wholewheat soaked in cold water overnight
salt and pepper

3 medium carrots, diced
2 medium leeks, sliced
4 oz (125g) cauliflower florets

*For the cheese sauce:*
2 oz (50g) vegetable margarine
2 oz (50g) wholemeal flour
1 pint (575ml) milk

4 oz (125g) Cheddar cheese, grated
salt and black pepper

2 oz (50g) Cheddar cheese, grated
2 oz (50g) wholemeal breadcrumbs

little chopped parsley

Cook the wheat in boiling salted water for 30–40 minutes until soft but not mushy.

Meanwhile, steam the vegetables, seasoned with salt and pepper, for 10–15 minutes until just tender.

Preheat your oven to 190°C/375°F/gas 5.

To make the cheese sauce, melt the margarine and add the flour to make a roux. Then off the heat gently add the milk, stirring all the while until the sauce thickens. Add the cheese and adjust the seasoning.

Drain wheat and combine with the vegetables and the cheese sauce. Sprinkle the breadcrumbs, cheese and parsley over the top and bake in the oven, on the shelf above centre, for 20 minutes until golden brown and bubbling. Serve hot.

---

## Coconut and Sultana Curry
*Serves 4*

*The Old Bakehouse, Castle Cary*
*Chef: Susan Roxburgh*

1 large onion, chopped
1 large cooking apple, chopped
  but not peeled
2 dessertspoons curry powder
4 oz (125g) sultanas
1 dessertspoon tomato purée
½ teaspoon ground ginger

2 oz (50g) desiccated coconut
2 teaspoons demerara sugar
juice 1 lemon
4 oz (125g) red lentils
1½ pints (875ml) vegetable stock
pinch salt

*This curry is delicious served with brown rice, sweet chutney and fruity side salads. I also add hard boiled eggs for a more substantial meal and for non-vegetarian friends, prawn or chicken may be added to a separate pan without much ado!*

Sauté the onion in the oil until soft.

Add the apple, curry powder and ginger and cook for a minute. Add the coconut, sultanas, purée, stock, sugar and salt and simmer for 30 minutes.

Meanwhile cook the lentils until mushy. Add the lentils to the curry with some of the liquid and the lemon and allow to stand for some hours, preferably overnight, to encourage all the flavours to infuse.

Re-heat and serve. Delicious!

---

# Diwana Vegetable Curry with Chapattis    *Serves 4*

*Diwana Bhel-Poori House, London*
*Chef: Mr Patel*

2 tablespoons oil
1 teaspoon mustard seeds
1 teaspoon cumin
1 pinch asofoetida
2 lb (900g) macedoine vegetables
1 small tin tomatoes

salt to taste
sugar to taste
green coriander leaves
curry powder to taste
8 oz (225g) Basmatti rice, pre-
soaked for 30 minutes

*For the chapattis:*
8 oz (225g) coarse chapatti flour
or 100% wholewheat flour

2 tablespoons oil
warm water to mix

Heat the oil in a large pan and add to the mustard seeds, cumin and asofoetida. Leave until the seeds pop and then add the vegetables. Stir them well and then add a little water. The quantity you add depends on the thickness of gravy you prefer, but add about ½ pint (275ml) to start with.

Add the tomatoes and then sugar and spices to taste. Leave to simmer with the pan covered for at least 30 minutes until the vegetables are cooked and the flavours infused.

Cook the pre-soaked rice according to the directions on the packet and serve accompanied with the chapattis.

To make the chapattis, add the oil to the flour and then enough warm water to give a malleable but not wet dough. Knead well and leave to rest for 1 hour. Divide the dough into even sized pieces and roll out into rounds. They can be small and fat or large and thin, it does not matter. Heat up a heavy frying pan until it is smoking. Place one chapatti in and cook until bubbles appear. Turn over and cook on the other side. Keep the cooked ones warm whilst frying the rest.

---

## Lentils au Gratin

*Serves 4*

*Pilgrims, Tunbridge Wells*
*Chef: Helen Potter*

| | |
|---|---|
| 1 large onion, finely chopped | 7 oz (200g) red lentils |
| 2 carrots, finely chopped | 4 oz (125g) Cheddar, grated |
| 2 sticks celery, finely chopped | 2 tablespoons wholemeal |
| 2 tablespoons oil | breadcrumbs |
| 1 pint (575ml) vegetable stock | salt and black pepper to taste |

*Crunchy, tasty and very popular.*

Sweat the vegetables in the oil for 5 minutes. Stir in the lentils and stock and simmer gently for about 45 minutes, taking care not to burn them.

Turn the lentil mixture into a well greased dish and top with the cheese and breadcrumbs. Bake in a hot oven for about 30 minutes until golden brown and crisp. Finish under the grill to make the top really golden if necessary.

# Lentil Flan

*Serves 4–6*

*Siop Y Chwarel (The Quarry Shop), Machynlleth*
*Chef: Judy Williams*

**For the pastry:**

8 oz (225g) 100% wholewheat
   flour
4 oz (125g) vegetable margarine

pinch sea salt
water to mix

**For the filling:**

6 oz (175g) split red lentils
2 large onions, chopped
1 clove garlic, chopped
a little oil
3 free range eggs

¼ pint (150ml) milk
ground black pepper and sea salt
herbes de Provence
4 oz (125g) cheese, grated

2 tomatoes to garnish

sprinkling paprika

Pre-heat oven to 210°C/425°F/gas 7.

Boil the lentils in a large saucepan of water for about 20 minutes until all the water has been absorbed.

Fry the onion and garlic in the oil gently until soft but not brown.

Make the pastry by adding salt to the flour and rubbing in the margarine until the mixture looks like breadcrumbs. Slowly mix in the water to make a soft dough – wholewheat pastry tends to be rather crumbly so it has to be well stuck together. Roll out on a floured surface. Oil a flan tin – 10″ (25cm) in diameter – very well to stop the pastry sticking. Line with the pastry.

Add the onions and garlic to the lentils and spoon into the flan case. Smooth over.

Beat the eggs, milk, salt, pepper and herbs together and pour into the case. Sprinkle with grated cheese and decorate with tomato slices. Sprinkle a little paprika over to give good flavour and colour.

Bake in oven at pre-heated temperature for 10 minutes to cook the pastry underneath. Then lower the temperature to 190–200°C/375–400°F/gas 5–6 for a further 20 minutes or until the top is set.

---

# Red Kidney Bean Chilli with Brown Rice    *Serves 6*

*Slenders, London*
*Chef: Michael O'Sullivan*

1½ lb (675g) red kidney beans, soaked overnight
2 onions, finely chopped
2 cloves garlic, finely chopped
3 fl. oz (75ml) oil
2 green or red peppers, cleaned and diced
1½ teaspoons chilli powder
1 teaspoon cumin seeds
3 fl. oz (75ml) tomato purée
salt
¼ pint (150ml) water
8 oz (225g) mushrooms
1 tablespoon flour
1 lb (450g) long grain brown rice
salt
3 oz (75g) butter

Drain the beans and cook in salted boiling water until tender.

Fry the onion and garlic gently for 5 minutes.

Add the beans, chilli powder, tomato purée, salt, cumin seeds and water. Cook for 45 minutes on a low heat.

Add the mushrooms. Mix the flour with a little water and stir into the mixture. Cook for a further 15 minutes.

Cook the brown rice in salted water for 45 minutes. Drain and pour into a dish. Mix in the butter and serve.

# Vegetarian Chilli Beans

*Serves 8*

*Cherry Orchard, London*
*Chef: Judy Senior*

1¼ cups raw kidney beans,
   soaked overnight
½ cup bulgar
½ cup tomato juice
2 cloves garlic, crushed
¾ cup onions, chopped
½ cup celery, chopped
½ cup carrots, chopped
½ cup green peppers, chopped
1 cup fresh tomatoes, chopped

juice ¼ lemon
½ teaspoon basil
½ teaspoon ground cumin
¼ teaspoon chilli powder, or
   more to taste
pinch cayenne, or more to taste
pinch salt and pepper
1½ tablespoons tomato purée
2 tablespoons olive oil
cheese and parsley to decorate

Cook the kidney beans till tender, about 1 hour, ensuring that the water is boiling and not just simmering.

Heat tomato juice to boiling and pour over the raw bulgar. Cover and leave for 15 minutes. The bulgar should still be crunchy.

Sauté the onions and garlic in the olive oil. Add the carrots, spices and seasoning. When the vegetables are almost cooked, add the green peppers. Cook till tender.

Combine all, including the remaining ingredients and the bulgar in tomato juice. Heat together gently.

Serve topped with cheese and parsley.

# 'Wot, No Beefburgers?'

*Ganesha, Axminster*
*Chefs: Fred and Penny Easton*

2 oz (50g) soya beans, soaked
    overnight
2 oz (50g) aduki beans, soaked
    overnight
2 oz (50g) brown rice
1 carrot, diced
1 stalk celery, finely chopped

1 small onion, finely chopped
1 teaspoon yeast extract
1 teaspoon shoyu
about 2 oz (50g) wholemeal
    breadcrumbs
little grated cheese (optional)
oil for frying

*This dish was devised in response to the cries of 'Wot, no beefburgers?' from those who occasionally stray, unwittingly, into our restaurant in the summer months. I hope you'll agree that these are tastier by far. They are easier to handle if cooked straight from the freezer. Replace the breadcrumbs with soya flour if you want to make them gluten free.*

Cook the aduki beans and soya beans together until very soft (about 45 minutes under pressure).

Cook the brown rice in a pan of water until tender.

Mash the beans and rice together. Stir in the carrot, onion and celery and then the yeast extract and shoyu. Finally add enough breadcrumbs to thicken the mixture and make it possible to form into about 6 flat 'burgers'. Coat each burger lightly with flour, place on greaseproof paper and freeze.

Fry each burger for about 5 minutes each side in a little hot oil. If you like, add grated cheese after turning.

Serve in a buttered wholemeal roll with lots of salad.

# Indian Chickpea Casserole

*Serves 4*

*Wholemeal Vegetarian Café, Streatham*
*Chef: David Martin*

1 medium onion, chopped
2 cloves garlic, crushed
1–2 teaspoons freshly ground
 coriander
½ teaspoon chilli powder
2 tablespoons oil

1 red pepper, seeded and diced
1 green pepper, seeded and diced
1 14 oz (400g) tin tomatoes
8 oz (225g) chick peas (soaked
 and pre-cooked soft)
salt and pepper

Fry the onion, garlic, coriander and chilli powder in the oil. Once the onion is soft add the diced pepper.

Add the tomatoes, salt and pepper and simmer for 20 minutes.

Add the chick peas and simmer for a further 10 minutes uncovered until the liquid has reduced and the casserole is thick. Serve on a bed of brown rice.

# Mediterranean Casserole

*Serves 4*

*On The Eighth Day, Manchester*
*Chef: John Leverton*

4 oz (125g) black-eyed beans
8 oz (225g) onions, finely
  chopped

1 tablespoon olive oil

*Selection of following vegetables to weigh 2 lb (1 kg) in total:*

mushrooms
peppers
aubergines
courgettes

carrots
celery
cauliflower

1 teaspoon basil
1 teaspoon mint
1–2 cloves garlic, crushed
1 large pinch black pepper
1 teaspoon salt

8 black olives, more if liked,
  stoned
5 fl. oz (150ml) tomato juice
5 fl. oz (150ml) red wine or red
  grape juice

Boil the beans in a pan of water until soft, about 45 minutes.

Fry the onions in the olive oil until tender. Prepare the rest of the vegetables and cut them into even sized pieces. They must be small enough to cook quickly, but not so small that they become mushy. Add the vegetables and seasoning to the onions and sauté for just a few minutes.

Add the olives, tomato juice, red wine and beans. Simmer for 30 minutes or until all the vegetables are just tender. Stir them from time to time to ensure that they cook evenly.

Serve with rice or pasta.

# Red Bean and Chick Pea Casserole

*Serves 4*

*Nuthouse, London*
*Chefs: Magdi Aboulnass and Abraham Nasr*

8 oz (225g) red kidney beans,
  cooked
6 oz (175g) chick peas, cooked
2 small onions, sliced
4 sticks celery, sliced
5 carrots, sliced
5 potatoes, cut into rough cubes

2 teaspoons curry powder
3 teaspoons mixed herbs
1 teaspoon salt
½ teaspoon pepper
3 teaspoons soya sauce
2 teaspoons tomato purée
¾ pint (425 ml) water

Fry the onion in a little oil until light brown. Add the curry powder and cook for a little longer, stirring from time to time.

Add the tomato purée, water, carrots, beans, peas, potato, celery and seasoning. Simmer for 20 minutes.

Add soya sauce and mixed herbs and cook for another 15 minutes. Adjust seasoning.

Serve piping hot with rice.

---

# Vegetable Casserole

*Serves 6*

*Herbs, Skipton*

1 small cauliflower
1 lb (450g) potatoes, thinly sliced
1 lb (450g) courgettes. cut into
  ½" (1cm) slices

8 oz (225g) mushrooms, sliced
3 medium onions, sliced
1 lb (450g) tomatoes, skinned
2 oz (50g) margarine

*For the cheese sauce:*

2 oz (50g) margarine
2 tablespoons wholemeal flour
1 pint (575ml) milk
salt and black pepper

pinch English mustard
8 oz (225g) Cheddar cheese,
  grated

2 oz (50g) Cheddar, grated
2 oz (50g) wholemeal
  breadcrumbs

*Vary the vegetables according to season. You will find that aubergines, broccoli and brussels sprouts are all very good used in this dish.*

Cook the cauliflower and courgettes in boiling water until just tender.

Boil the potatoes for 3–4 minutes until slightly tender.

Fry the onions in the margarine. Add the mushrooms and tomatoes and cook for a few minutes.

To make the cheese sauce, melt the margarine and stir in the flour and cook slightly. Take off the heat and gradually stir in the milk. Return to the heat, bring to the boil and season. Add the grated cheese and cook just long enough to melt it.

Put all the vegetables into a large casserole dish. Pour over the cheese sauce and mix together, taking care not to break any of the vegetables. Sprinkle with grated cheese and breadcrumbs.

Place in the oven at 180°C/350°F/gas 4 for about 1 hour until the topping is golden brown and crunchy.

# Butter Bean Pie

*Serves 6*

*Good Food Café, Llandrindod Wells*
*Chefs: Heather Williams*

8 oz (225g) butter beans, soaked
   overnight
2 large onions, chopped
1 green pepper, chopped
1 heaped tablespoon tomato
   purée

1 heaped tablespoon brown sugar
1 teaspoon oregano
salt and pepper
14 oz (400g) tin tomatoes,
   roughly chopped

*For the topping:*
4 oz (125g) grated cheese
1 beaten egg

8 oz (225g) cottage cheese
salt and pepper

Boil the beans until soft but unbroken.

Fry the onion and green pepper in a little oil for 2 to 3 minutes. Add the tomatoes, the tomato purée, sugar, oregano and season well. Simmer until the vegetables are quite soft.

Strain the beans and save the liquid.

Mix all the ingredients in a 2 pint (generous litre) casserole. If necessary add some of the strained bean juice so that all the beans are covered.

Mix the topping ingredients together and spread over the mixture in the casserole. Cook until golden brown and bubbly at 180–190°C/ 350–375°F/gas 4–5.

This scrumptious dish is equally good using cannellini beans, which are very succulent. Any leftovers can be used as a tasty filling for a quiche.

# Brussels Sprout and Chestnut Pie

*Country Kitchen, Southsea*
*Chef: Jean Piper*

*For the pastry:*

1 lb (450g) 85% wheatmeal flour
8 oz (225g) margarine
1 egg

1 teaspoon salt
¼ pint (150ml) water

*For the filling:*

1 lb (450g) brussels sprouts
8 oz (225g) dried chestnuts
1 large potato, peeled and
   chopped into 1″ cubes
1 large onion, roughly chopped
1 leek, roughly chopped
8 oz (225g) mushrooms,
   quartered

2 oz (50g) margarine
4 oz (125g) 100% wholemeal
   flour
1 tablespoon ground cumin
½ teaspoon nutmeg
1 teaspoon mixed herbs
1 pint (575ml) milk
sea salt and pepper

beaten egg and milk, mixed to make a glaze

Cook the chestnuts in a pan of water for 45 minutes, then remove any black remnants of skin.

Boil the potatoes until tender.

Melt the margarine in a large saucepan with the herbs and spices. Stir in the flour and gradually add the milk. Bring to the boil and cook for 2–3 minutes, stirring well. Put to one side.

Sauté the onions, leeks and mushrooms in a little fat until tender. Add them to the sauce with the brussels sprouts, chestnuts and potato. Season with salt and pepper to taste.

To make the pastry, rub the margarine into the flour until it forms a crumb-like mixture. Add the salt and then the egg and enough water to bind the pastry together.

Pour the sauce mixture into a shallow ovenproof dish. Roll out the pastry thickly and place over the top of the dish. Flute the edge and brush the top with the egg and milk glaze.

Bake at 175°C/300°F/gas 3 for about 20 minutes until the pastry is cooked and the filling heated through.

---

# Courgette and Cheese Pie

*Serves 4–6*

*Healthy, Wealthy and Wise, London*
*Chef: Kath*

*For the dough:*
8 oz (225g) wholewheat flour
½ oz (12g) fresh yeast

¼ pint (150ml) water
mixed, chopped fresh herbs

*For the filling:*
8 courgettes, sliced
2 carrots, sliced
½ swede, peeled and sliced
14 oz (400g) tin tomatoes

8 oz (225g) Cheddar, grated
pinch asofoetida (if available)
butter for frying

Prepare the dough by heating the water to blood heat and to it add the fresh yeast. Cream it until it dissolves and add to the flour with the herbs. Draw the mixture to a dough, adding more water if necessary and knead well. Cover and leave in a warm place until it has doubled in size – about 1 hour.

Simmer the vegetables in a little butter until tender. Add the tomatoes, cheese and asofoetida, mix well and then pour into a casserole dish. Check seasoning.

Knead the risen dough lightly. Roll out into strips and make a lattice work on top of the vegetables. Place in the oven for about 30 minutes at 180°C/350°F/gas 4 until the dough is risen and well cooked.

---

## Gloucester Pie

*Cheese Press, Crickhowell*
*Chef: Mrs Morgan-Grenville*

8 slices buttered bread
4 oz (125g) Double Gloucester
   cheese, thinly sliced
8 oz (225g) tomatoes, skinned
   and thinly sliced

¼ pint (150ml) milk
1 egg
1 level teaspoon made mustard
salt and pepper
1 oz (25g) butter

Remove the crusts from the bread and sandwich together in pairs with the sliced cheese and tomato. Cut each sandwich into 4 triangles and arrange in a shallow, buttered dish.

Beat the milk with the egg, mustard and seasoning. Pour this mixture over the sandwiches and leave until the bread has absorbed all the liquid, about 30 minutes. Dot the top with knobs of butter.

Bake at 190°C/375°F/gas 5 for 20–30 minutes or until the top is crisp and brown.

# Mushroom and Goat's Cheese Pie

*Serves 8*

*Good Earth, Wells*
*Chef: Tina Dearling*

*For the pastry:*

8 oz (225g) 100% wholewheat flour

4 oz (125g) butter
water to mix

*For the filling:*

2 oz (50g) butter
12 oz (350g) mushrooms, sliced
1 onion, chopped
juice ½ lemon
salt and black pepper

dash Worcester sauce
1 teaspoon chives, chopped
1 teaspoon parsley, chopped
1 clove garlic, crushed

*For the white sauce:*

2 oz (50g) butter
2 heaped tablespoons flour
1 pint milk

1 bay leaf
salt and black pepper

4 oz (125g) soft goat's cheese

To make the pastry, rub the butter into the flour until it resembles breadcrumbs. Add water until you have a pliable dough. Roll out onto a floured board and line an 8" flan case with half of the pastry.

Sauté the onion and mushrooms lightly in butter. Add the lemon juice, salt and pepper, Worcester sauce, chives, parsley and garlic.

To make the white sauce, melt the butter, add the flour and cook gently until it froths. Remove from heat and gently add the milk, stirring all the time. Add the bay leaf, return to the heat and stir until thickened. Season and simmer for about 15 minutes.

Melt the goat's cheese in the white sauce.

Add the mushroom mixture to the cheese sauce and pour into the pastry case. Roll out the remaining pastry, place it on top of the pie and decorate with pastry leaves. Glaze the top with egg or milk and bake at 200°C/400°F/gas 6 for 20–30 minutes until the pastry is crisp and golden.

---

# Shepherd's Pie

*Serves 6*

*Good Food Café, Llandrindod Wells*
*Chef: Heather Williams*

8 oz (225g) brown or green lentils, pre-soaked
8 oz (225g) carrots, finely chopped
8 oz (225g) swede, finely chopped
4 sticks celery, finely chopped
1 lb (450g) onions, finely chopped

2 tablespoons tomato purée
2 tablespoons tamari or soya sauce
salt and pepper
oil to fry
3 lb (1.5kg) potatoes, cooked and mashed

*You will find that this dish is equally successful if you use vegetables according to season.*

Cook the lentils in a pan of water until soft.

Fry the chopped vegetables in oil until tender, adding the tamari part of the way through cooking.

Combine the vegetables with the cooked lentils, tomato purée and enough lentil juice to keep the mixture moist, as for a traditional Shepherd's Pie. Season well and place in a buttered casserole.

Cover with the mashed potatoes and cook at 180°C/350°F/gas 4 for about 30 minutes until golden brown.

# Spring Vegetable Pie

*Serves 6*

*The Old Bakehouse, Castle Cary*
*Chef: Susan Roxburgh*

2 onions, chopped
2 tablespoons sunflower oil
1 lb (450g) new potatoes, washed
    and cubed but not peeled

1 teaspoon mixed herbs

*A selection of the following:*
new carrots, chopped
green pepper, sliced

4 oz (125g) button mushrooms
2 leeks

Jerusalem artichokes

white cabbage, shredded

salt and black pepper
¼ pint (150ml) cheese sauce

8 oz (225g) shortcrust pastry
    (made with 81% wholemeal
    flour)

*I wait for the first new potatoes to appear before making this pie.*

Sauté the onion in the oil until soft. Add the potatoes and the mixed herbs. Add the rest of the vegetables. Sauté gently in a covered pan until the potatoes are just cooked. Season with salt and black pepper.

Fold the vegetables into your cheese sauce.

Line a pie dish with the pastry, pour in the vegetables and cover with a pastry lid.

Bake at 190°C/375°F/gas 5 for 35 minutes.

Serve with a jug of cheese sauce.

# Sweets

## Almond Semolina

*Diwana Bhel-Poori House, London*
*Chef: Mr Patel*

6 oz (175g) semolina
2½ tablespoons ghee
¾–1 pint (425–575ml) milk

2–3 oz (50–75g) whole blanched
   almonds
sugar to taste

Heat the ghee in a heavy frying pan. Add the semolina and heat, stirring until it turns a golden brown colour. The semolina should absorb all the ghee and begin to look like crumbs.

Take the pan off the heat and gradually add about ¾ pint (425ml) of the milk, stirring continuously. Add enough to make the mixture wet. Return to the heat until semolina absorbs all the moisture. Add the sugar to taste and sprinkle over the blanched almonds.

Serve piping hot, immediately – if you allow it to stand it will thicken up and become stodgy; if this happens add a little more milk and heat through, stirring well.

# Apricot Slice

*Siop Y Chwarel (The Quarry Shop), Machynlleth*
*Chefs: Anne Lowmass and Helen Allen*

8 oz (225g) dried apricots
8 oz (225g) margarine
4 oz (125g) muscovado sugar

12 oz (350g) wholemeal flour
6 oz (175g) porridge oats
½ teaspoon salt

Put the apricots in a pan and add enough water to just cover them. Boil, stirring occasionally, adding more water if necessary until it forms a spreadable purée – about 30 minutes.

Melt the margarine, add the sugar and stir until it dissolves. Add to the flour, oats and salt, mixing with your hands until the mixture resembles breadcrumbs.

Press half the crumb mixture into an oiled flat tray and cover with apricot purée. Put the rest of the crumbs on top and press down evenly.

Bake at 180°C/350°F/gas 4 for about 30 minutes or until golden brown. Allow to cool and cut into slices before serving.

---

# Apple and Blackberry Charlotte

*Serves 4*

*Slenders, London*
*Chef: Michael O'Sullivan*

1½ lb (675g) cooking apples
juice and rind 1 lemon
2 oz (50g) brown sugar
4 oz (125g) margarine

slices wholewheat bread
8 oz (225g) fresh frozen
    blackberries
1 teaspoon cinnamon

Cut the apples and stew with the lemon juice, sugar and a little water. Pass through a sieve.

Melt the margarine, dip each piece of bread in it and line the bottom and sides of a 6″ (16cm) soufflé dish with most of the bread.

Place the apple purée and blackberries in the dish. Sprinkle the cinnamon over the fruit.

Cover with more slices of bread and then some foil. Bake in a moderate oven until the bread is crisp and brown.

---

# Apple Kanten                                    *Serves 4–6*

*Natural Snack, London*
*Chef: Bretta Carthey*

| | |
|---|---|
| 4 medium sized sweet eating apples, sliced | agar agar flakes – follow instructions on packet for quantity |
| 1 oz (25g) raisins | |
| 24 fl. oz (850ml) apple juice | strawberries to decorate |

Cook the apples and raisins in the apple juice until soft.

Purée the mixture and return it to the heat. Sprinkle in the agar agar flakes and stir in well, making sure that the flakes have dissolved. Simmer for 5 minutes.

Slice the strawberries and arrange them on the bottom of a slightly wetted shallow baking pan. Pour the apple purée on top and leave to set.

To serve, turn the mould upside down onto a serving plate and cut the kanten into attractive shapes.

# Apricot and Banana Purée

*Serves 4*

*Cranks, London*

12 oz (350g) dried apricots, soaked in water overnight
2 ripe bananas, chopped
4 tablespoons cream or 4 tablespoons skimmed milk powder

1–2 teaspoons honey
fruit juice, if required
chopped walnuts for decoration

Put the soaked apricots, chopped bananas and cream in a blender. Whizz for several minutes, adding a little fruit juice if the mixture is too thick.

Pour the purée into individual glasses, chill and decorate with the chopped walnuts.

---

# Apricot and Yoghurt Pie

*Wholemeal Vegetarian Café, Streatham*
*Chef: David Martin*

4 oz (125g) sweetened wholemeal pastry
6 oz (175g) apricots, soaked overnight and cooked till soft

3 eggs
½ pint (275ml) natural yoghurt
2–3 tablespoons honey
nutmeg, freshly grated

Roll out the pastry and line an 8–9″ flan ring. Bake blind at 170°C/325°F/gas 3 for about 20 minutes or until the pastry is cooked. Remove the baking beans for the last 5 minutes of the cooking time to allow the bottom to crisp up.

Distribute the apricots evenly over the base. Combine the egg, yoghurt and honey together and mix well. Pour this mixture over the apricots. Sprinkle the top liberally with nutmeg and return to the oven for about 30 minutes until the filling has set. Serve warm or cold.

---

# Banana Cream Whip

*Serves 6*

*Country Kitchen, Southsea*
*Chef: Jean Piper*

2 lb (1kg) bananas, mashed
2 lemons, grated and juiced

½ pint (225ml) double cream

*For decoration:*
6 twists lemon
6 strips angelica

nuts, chopped and roasted
½ pint (225ml) double cream

Add the grated lemon rind and the juice to the mashed bananas. Then add the cream and whip until thick and frothy.

Put into individual glasses. Chill until ready to serve.

Whip up the cream and pipe a rosette on top of each portion. Finish by decorating with a twist of lemon, angelica and the nuts.

# Fried Banana Split

*Huckleberry's, Bath*
*Chef: Rob Craven*

1 firm banana
1 tablespoon whipped cream
1 tablespoon roasted nuts,
    crushed (walnuts or peanuts or
    mixed)

1 dessertspoon maple syrup
1 tablespoon crushed 'Flake'
    chocolate bar
butter

Peel and cut the banana lengthways. Fry in the butter on a medium heat. Cook each side for 2 minutes.

Serve immediately: put the banana on a plate, with the flat surface down so that they bracket the centre of the plate. Onto the centre area of the plate, put the whipped cream and sprinkle with the nuts and chocolate. Lastly pour over the maple syrup and eat. Delicious.

---

# Cashew and Fruit 'Ice Cream'

*On The Eighth Day, Manchester*
*Chef: John Leverton – variations by other members*

6 oz (175g) cashew nuts
½ pint (275ml) pineapple juice

honey to sweeten

Put the juice and nuts in a blender and mix until smooth and slightly thicker than single cream.

Taste and sweeten with honey. It should be over-sweet as the sweetness is less evident when frozen.

Pour the mixture into a shallow dish and freeze. It's as easy as that!

A whole range of flavours can be made and some suggestions are given below. The basic rule is that there should be equal volumes of nuts and juice.

(a)  honey, water and vanilla

(b)  maple syrup – VERY good, but expensive

(c)  grape juice

(d)  puréed fruit – bananas are good and reasonably cheap

(e)  stir nuts and raisins into the ice cream when it's frozen

---

# Chestnut and Banana Sundae
*Serves 4*

*Delany's, Shrewsbury*
*Chefs: Odette and Belinda*

15 oz (425g) natural unsweetened chestnut purée or equivalent fresh chestnuts, boiled and peeled
2 bananas
lemon juice, to taste

honey to taste
½ pint (275ml) whipping or double cream, whipped stiffish
banana slices to garnish
single cream to garnish

Liquidise the purée or whole chestnuts with the bananas.

Add the lemon juice and honey to taste – not too much honey though, it easily becomes too sweet.

Fold in the whipped cream and taste again.

If there is any left at this stage, dollop it into individual glasses, with slices of banana between dollops and finish with a generous dribble of cream on top.

---

## Chocolate and Raisin Pie

*Serves 4*

*Clinchs Salad House, Chichester*
*Chef: Mrs A. Ellis*

½ pint (275ml) milk
2½ oz (60g) sugar
2 oz (50g) dark cooking chocolate
1½ oz (35g) cocoa
1 oz (25g) cornflour

2 oz (50g) raisins, soaked in 2
   teaspoons rum
6 oz (175g) shortcrust pastry
whipped cream and chocolate
   curls to decorate

Line a 7" loose bottomed flat tin with the pastry. Leave to rest and then bake blind until a nice pale brown.

Mix the cornflour with a little of the milk to make a paste.

Put the rest of the milk in a saucepan with the cocoa, chocolate and sugar. Stir over a gentle heat until melted. Add the cornflour paste, stirring all the time until it thickens. Add the raisins and pour the mixture into the flan case. Leave to cool and set.

When cold and ready to serve spread or pipe whipped cream over and decorate with curls of chocolate.

# Wholewheat Choux Pastry Profiteroles

*Serves 6*

*Hockneys, Croydon*
*Chef: Tony Bowall*

½ pint (275ml) milk
4 oz (125g) butter
5 oz (150g) wholewheat flour,
　sieved

4 eggs
pinch salt and sugar

*For the chocolate sauce:*
2 oz (50g) butter
2 tablespoons drinking chocolate
1 dessertspoon sugar
¼ pint (150ml) milk

1 dessertspoon cornflour,
　dissolved in 1 dessertspoon
　water

½ pint (275ml) double cream, for the filling

*You can vary the filling by replacing the cream with a mixture of coffee and cream or chocolate and cream.*

Boil the milk, water, butter and sugar together in a pan until the butter melts. Remove from the heat and mix in the flour and salt all at once. Return to a low heat and beat with a wooden spoon until the mixture leaves the sides of the pan in one piece. Allow to cool slightly.

Add the eggs, one by one, mixing them in well after each addition. (If you add the eggs when the mixture is very hot they will scramble and go lumpy.) When the mixture is smooth and shiny, place in a forcing bag with a plain nozzle and pipe on to a dampened baking sheet in walnut-sized balls of 3″ (8cm) length – these will make eclairs. Bake at 220°C/425°F/gas 7 for 20 minutes. Then pierce with a knife to release the steam and dry them out at 180°C/350°F/gas 4 for 10–15 minutes.

131

Allow to cool completely and then fill them with the double cream, which you have whipped.

Make the chocolate sauce by combining the butter, drinking chocolate and sugar over a low heat. Carefully whisk in the milk and finally add the liquid cornflour and cook until the sauce thickens to a coating consistency.

Serve the sauce hot and pour it over a mountain of profiteroles just before taking it to the table.

---

## Spicy Date Tart

Serves 6

*Pilgrims, Tunbridge Wells*
*Chef: Joanna Bowyer*

1 lightly pre-baked 9″ (23cm)
   shortcrust flan case
12 oz (350g) dates, chopped
4 eggs, lightly beaten
1 pint (575g) single or whipping
   cream

¼ teaspoon salt
2 teaspoons cinnamon
½ teaspoon ground nutmeg
¼ teaspoon ground cloves
2 oz (50g) fresh breadcrumbs
2 oz (50g) desiccated coconut

*Very popular with our customers, the rich filling is spicily delicious and has no sugar in it. As fast as we bake them, they seem to vanish!*

Line the pastry case with the chopped dates.

Beat the eggs, cream, salt and spices and stir into the crumbs.

Pour the egg mixture over the dates and bake at 190°C/375°F/gas 5 for about 15 minutes or until set. Sprinkle over the coconut and return to a slower oven, 180°C/350°F/gas 4 for another 15 minutes.

Remove from the oven and cool before cutting. To make it extra rich, serve with whipped cream.

# Wholemeal Date and Toffee Pudding

*Serves 6*

*The Old Bakehouse, Castle Cary*
*Chef: Susan Roxburgh*

6 oz (175g) dates, chopped
4 oz (125g) good margarine
5 oz (150g) demerara sugar
1 teaspoon vanilla essence
1 egg

4 oz (125g) self-raising flour
4 oz (125g) 100% wholemeal
  flour
1 teaspoon baking powder

*For the toffee sauce:*
3 oz (75g) margarine
5 oz (150g) soft brown sugar

2 tablespoons whipped cream

*Wickedly full of calories, but irresistible!*

Pour ½ pint (275ml) water over the dates and leave to stand.

Cream the margarine and sugar until soft and add the egg and vanilla essence and beat well. Add the self-raising flour, wholemeal flour and the baking powder which will make rather a stiff mixture. Add the dates and water turning the mixture into a thin batter.

Pour into a greased, oval Pyrex dish, about 4" deep and bake at 180°C/ 375°F/gas 5 for 45 minutes.

Make the sauce by melting the margarine with the brown sugar in a non-stick pan. Add the whipped cream, stir well and do not boil the mixture. Pour this sauce over the pudding and return to the oven for 15 minutes.

Serve with whipped cream.

# Fruit Compôte

*Nature's Way, Eastbourne*
*Chefs: Maurice and Dorothy Fossitt*

8 oz (225g) fresh blackberries,
   frozen if unavailable
8 oz (225g) fresh blackcurrants,
   frozen if unavailable

8 oz (225g) fresh gooseberries,
   frozen if unavailable
8 oz (225g) dried apricots,
   washed and soaked overnight

*The success of this sweet is in its presentation as well as the variety of flavours. The fruits are cooked separately so that they retain their colour.*

Cook the soaked apricots gently until soft and sweeten to taste with demerara sugar.

Poach the blackberries, blackcurrants and gooseberries gently in separate pans of water until they are soft and the fruit is unbroken. Sweeten to taste with soft brown sugar. Leave to cool.

When cold strain the apricots and gooseberries, their juices are not used.

Using a half quantity of each, layer the fruit into a glass bowl as follows: apricots first, then blackberries and blackcurrants with some of their juices and finally the gooseberries. Taste and add more sugar if required. Repeat with the rest of the fruit, keeping back a few apricots and gooseberries to blend together for the top.

Serve cold with single cream.

# Fruit Cream

Serves 4

*Stanards, Canterbury*
*Chef: Jacky Luckhurst*

1 apple, cored and chopped
1 orange, peeled and chopped
1 banana, peeled and chopped
4 oz (125g) grapes, depipped

1 oz (25g) raisins
8 fl. oz (225ml) whipping cream
desiccated coconut and slices of
    fruit to decorate

Put all the fruit in a liquidiser with the raisins and cream and whizz until evenly blended.

Put into individual glasses and decorate with a sprinkling of coconut and slices of fruit.

---

# Dried Fruit and Soured Cream

Serves 4

*Henderson's Salad Table, Edinburgh*
*Chef: Janet Henderson*

8 oz (225g) dried fruit – any
    mixture of apples, prunes,
    apricot, peaches, figs – soaked
    overnight
1   cooking apple, quartered,
    cored and roughly chopped

2 oz (50g) stem ginger in syrup,
    finely chopped
5 fl. oz (150ml) soured cream

Mix the apple, dried fruits, half the ginger and all the syrup together. Place in a glass serving dish.

Pour over the soured cream and decorate with the remaining ginger.

# Fresh Fruit Slice

*Food For Health, London*
*Chef: John Cross*

Enough of your favourite pastry to line and cover a shallow baking
dish

| | |
|---|---|
| eating apples, cored and sliced but not peeled | 1 banana, sliced |
| oranges, peeled and cubed | handful grapes, halved and depipped |

*This is really a do it yourself dish which can be varied according to season
and preference. In season use strawberries, raspberries, pitted cherries,
peaches, pears, melon (only a little or it will make the pastry soggy), plums
or any of the small orange family. You can serve the slice hot or cold with
custard, cream, yoghurt or ice cream. It will rarely need sweetening but
add some honey if you think it necessary. Be careful to cut the fruit into
small enough pieces to pack solidly in the pastry.*

Line the dish with the pastry and leave to one side.

Mix the fruits together and place on the pastry. You will need enough
fruit to come level with the top of the dish.

Cover with a pastry lid and bake in the oven at 200°C/400°F/gas 5 for
20 minutes. Then lower the heat to 180° C/375°F/gas 5 and continue
cooking until the pastry is brown and crisp and the fruit cooked.

# Gooseberry and Apple Crumble

*Serves 4–6*

*Harvest, London*
*Chef: Giuseppe Rossi*

8 oz (225g) gooseberries
8 oz (225g) cooking apples,
   peeled, cored and sliced

*For the crumble:*

4 oz (125g) honey
4 oz (125g) margarine
8 oz (225g) oatflakes
2 oz (50g) wheatmeal flour

1 oz (25g) raisins
1 oz (25g) dessicated coconut
1 tablespoon sugar

Melt the margarine and honey in a pan over a low heat. Mix in the oats and then the flour.

Place a layer of the mixture on the bottom of a baking dish. Cover with half the gooseberries and sliced apple and then sprinkle over the raisins and coconut.

Repeat with more crumble and fruit and finally a layer of crumble. Sprinkle the sugar over the top and bake it 180°C/350°F/gas 4 for about 30 minutes.

# Lemon Mousse

*Serves 8*

*The Old Bakehouse, Castle Cary*
*Chef: Susan Roxburgh*

| | |
|---|---|
| 7 eggs, separated | 8 oz (225g) caster sugar |
| 2 dessertspoons gelatine or | 2 large or 3 small lemons |
|    equivalent agar agar | 6 dessertspoons water |

*The advantage of this lovely, lemony sweet is that it contains no cream and is as light as a feather.*

Beat the egg yolks and the sugar until thick and creamy.

Mix the gelatine and the water in a small basin and stand in a pan of water on the stove. Stir occasionally until the gelatine is completely dissolved and has become clear. Cool.

Grate the rind of the lemons and squeeze the juice.

Beat the egg whites until stiff.

When the gelatine is cool but not set add it together with the juice and rind to the yolk and sugar mixture. Fold in the whites gently and pour the mousse into one large or two smaller soufflé dishes. Pop into the fridge to set.

# Mincemeat Flan

*Good Food Café, Llandrindod Wells*
*Chef: Sue Early*

2 apples, peeled, cored and
    grated
6 oz (175g) mincemeat

1 tablespoon lemon juice
2 oz (50g) flaked almonds
5 fl. oz (150ml) whipped cream

*For the pastry:*
6 oz (175g) plain flour
2 oz (50g) ground almonds

4 oz (125g) margarine
water to mix

Make the pastry. Wrap in cling film and place in the fridge for 1 hour.

Roll out the pastry and line an 8" (20cm) flan case.

Put the apples into the pastry case and cover with the mincemeat and sprinkle with lemon juice.

Bake at 200°C/400°F/gas 6 for 15 minutes then lower to 170°C/325°F/gas 3 for 10 minutes. Cool well.

When the flan is completely cool, whip the cream and smooth over the mincemeat. Sprinkle the almonds on top ready to serve.

# Orange and Brandy Pancakes

*Nettles, Cambridge*
*Chef: Mary Anne Marks*

*For the butter:*

4 oz (125g) wholewheat flour

1 egg

pinch salt

½ pint (275ml) milk

*For the sauce:*

juice 2 oranges

2 tablespoons brown sugar

2 fl. oz (50ml) brandy (more if you like!)

½ teaspoon orange peel, finely grated

Make the batter by gradually adding the egg and then the milk to the salt and flour until the mixture is pourable but not too thin. Mix well to disperse any lumps.

Heat the oil in a small frying pan and cook the pancakes – the mixture should make about 8, 7″ pancakes. As you fry keep the cooked pancakes warm on a plate over a pan of hot water.

Fold the pancakes up and arrange on a warm serving dish.

Make the sauce by heating the orange juice with the sugar until it bubbles. Add the brandy, remove from the heat and pour over the pancakes, covering them evenly with sauce. To finish off, sprinkle over a little orange peel and serve.

# Pashka

*Marno's, Ipswich*
*Chef: Ferial Rogers*

| | |
|---|---|
| 1 large egg | 3 oz (75g) seedless raisins |
| 2 oz (50g) soft brown sugar | grated rind 1 orange |
| 1 lb (450g) curd cheese | 5 fl. oz (150ml) double cream |

*This is a very rich Russian dessert which is served largely during their Easter festivities.*

Beat the egg and sugar together to a thick cream.

Mix the raisins, curd cheese and orange rind in well.

Half whip the cream, then fold in the cheese mixture very thoroughly until there are no lumps left.

Place in one large or four individual dishes. Chill and eat!

---

# Payasam

*Serves 4*

*Ganesha, Axminster*
*Chef: Fred and Penny Easton*

| | |
|---|---|
| 4 oz (125g) yellow split peas, soaked at least for 1 hour | 4 cardamom pods, white or green |
| 1 coconut or 6 oz (175g) desiccated | 1 oz (25g) cashew nuts |
| | 1 oz (25g) sultanas |
| 4 oz (125g) jaggeri (Indian palm sugar) – or 2 oz (50g) demerara and 2 oz (50g) muscovado | little ghee or sunflower oil |
| | chopped banana or pineapple to make the payasam special |

*This is one version of a very popular south Indian sweet. It is cooked on festive days and an offering is made before it is eaten. The recipe came to me from some dear friends in Kersala who taught me much about cooking with love and devotion and serving God first, not to mention the delights of the Indian cuisine. Payasam may be eaten hot or cold. Make it more special by mixing in the chopped banana or pineapple.*

Cook the yellow split peas in twice their volume of water until they disintegrate – about 10 minutes under pressure. They should be a thick mush.

Make the coconut milk by grating or grinding the coconut flesh. Add 1 cup warm water and squeeze the coconut with your hand for a few minutes. 'Wring out' the coconut and place in a bowl. Strain the liquid into another bowl – this is the first milk.

Add another cup of water to the coconut and repeat the squeezing and strain the liquid into a separate bowl. Repeat the operation once more, adding the third milk to the second.

Melt the jaggeri slowly in a heavy saucepan. When completely melted add the second and third coconut milks and the yellow split peas and cook until the mixture thickens. This may take quite a long time, so be patient, but the mixture should be the consistency of a thick sauce.

Split the cardamom pods open and grind the seeds. Add them to the jaggeri mixture when it is almost ready.

Sauté the cashew nuts and sultanas gently in a little ghee until they turn brown. Add to the payasam with the first milk (and the fruit if desired) just before serving.

# Pineapple Jelly Tart

*Serves 4–6*

*Grapevine, Birmingham*
*Chef: Pat Gully*

1 pineapple, cut into small
   wedges
½ pint (275ml) fresh orange juice

2 teaspoons honey
1½ teaspoons agar agar

*For the pastry:*
6 oz (175g) 100% organic
   stoneground wholewheat flour
1 egg

2 fl. oz (50ml) sunflower oil
2 fl. oz (50ml) water

*This is a marvellously versatile sweet – you can substitute the pineapple for bananas, wafer thin slices of apple, oranges, apricots, plums, damsons, strawberries, blackberries, gooseberries, prunes, cherries, pears, in fact anything that takes your fancy, either stewed or raw as is best. You can use apple juice instead of orange juice and the pastry can be used for a savoury cheese flan base!*

Mix all the pastry ingredients. Add a touch more water if too dry. Chill for 30 minutes before rolling out and pressing into a flan case. Bake blind in the oven at 200°C/400°F/gas 6 for 15–20 minutes.

Arrange the pineapple wedges in a close pattern in the flan case.

In a small saucepan boil the orange juice with the honey and agar agar, stirring occasionally. Leave to cool for a few minutes.

Pour the cooled orange juice over the pineapple and leave to set in the fridge.

# Fresh Cream Raspberry Meringue

*Food For Thought, Sherborne*
*Chefs: Michael and Margaret Balfour*

4 eggs whites
8 oz (225g) raw cane demerara
   sugar, finely ground in coffee
   grinder or liquidiser

½ pint (275ml) double cream
8 oz (225g) raspberries
chopped almonds to decorate

*This is a very impressive looking dessert. The meringues can be made well in advance and stored in an airtight container. At the restaurant, customers often ask for a piece to be reserved for them before they have even considered a first course! Use other fruit for variety – strawberries, peaches or dried fruits such as apricots which you have soaked and cooked. Egg whites freeze, so never throw any away! Save them for meringues.*

Whisk the egg whites until they are stiff, such that if you were to turn the bowl upside down they would stay put.

Whisk in the sugar.

Draw two 8″ (20cm) circles on non-stick baking paper placed on baking sheets. Spread the meringue mixture evenly over the two circles.

Leave in an oven preheated to 100°C/200°F/gas ¼ overnight (10–12 hours) until they are completely dried out. They will be ready when it is easy to peel the paper away from the meringues. Leave to cool.

Whip the cream and spread part of it on top of one meringue and cover with most of the raspberries. Put the second meringue on top and decorate with the remaining cream and raspberries. Add chopped almonds for extra decoration.

# Raspberry Dream

*Serves 6*

*Mother Nature, Stroud*
*Chef: Cindy*

8 oz (225g) fresh raspberries or 1
   tin drained raspberries
½ pint (275ml) double cream
½ pint (275ml) natural yoghurt

2 tablespoons light brown sugar
1 tablespoon fresh lemon juice
2 teaspoons agar agar dissolved in
   ½ cup raspberry juice or water

Blend the raspberries, lemon juice, agar agar and sugar together.

Whip the cream until fairly stiff and stir into it the fruit and yoghurt. Place in individual dishes or one large bowl and pop into the fridge to set.

To serve, decorate with raspberries or slivered almonds and cinnamon.

---

# Revani

*Serves 4*

*Harvest, Ambleside*
*Chef: Gillian Kelly*

9 eggs
6 oz (175g) sugar
pinch salt
4½ oz (135g) 85% wheatmeal
   flour

4½ oz (135g) ground almonds
grated rind and juice 1 lemon or
   orange
1 teaspoon baking powder
grated rind and juice of 1 orange

*For the syrup:*
6 oz (175g) sugar

½ pint (275ml) water

*This is a recipe that I brought back from Turkey after having lived there for four years which has been adapted by Gill Delaney our super home baker of wholemeal bread and cakes.*

Separate the eggs. Beat the yolks with the sugar.

Beat the whites with a pinch of salt until stiff.

Mix together the yolks and whites and then add the flour, almonds, lemon or orange rind and juice and the baking powder.

Place in a greased cake tin and cook in a fairly hot oven, 180°C/350°F/gas 4 for about 20 minutes. Turn out and cool on a wire rack.

Return the sponge to a high sided cake tin. To make syrup, dissolve sugar in the water and then add orange rind and juice. Pour this hot syrup over sponge and leave for several hours before serving with whipped cream.

---

# Rhubarb and Almond Tart

*Serves 6*

*Cheese Press, Crickhowell*
*Chef: Mrs Morgan-Grenville*

| | |
|---|---|
| 6 oz (175g) shortcrust pastry | 4 oz (125g) butter |
| 2 lb (1kg) rhubarb, chopped into thick, even sized chunks | 4 oz (125g) sugar |
| | 4 oz (125g) flaked almonds |
| sweetening to taste | 2 eggs |

Make the pastry and line an 8–9″ (20–22cm) flan dish.

Sweeten the chopped rhubarb and arrange on the bottom of the flan case.

Cream the butter and sugar together. Beat in the eggs and fold in the almonds.

Spread the almond mixture over the fruit – which will stick through unevenly. Bake at 180°C/350°F/gas 4 for about 20 minutes until the top is brown and crisp looking.

---

# Gannets Boozy Trifle
*Serves 8 hungry people*

*Gannets, Newark*
*Chef: Hilary Bower*

1½ large jam Swiss rolls, cut into slices
¼ pint (150ml) medium sweet sherry
2 oz (50g) broken meringue pieces or 4oz (125g) macaroons
16 oz (500g) tin raspberries or strawberries

4 egg yolks, whisked
2 oz (50g) sugar
1 pint (575ml) creamy milk
large tot brandy
½ pint (275ml) whipping cream
macaroons and chocolate flake to decorate

*This dish improves with keeping, so can be made the day before and topped with cream just before serving.*

To make the base of the trifle, layer slices of Swiss roll, meringue or macaroon, raspberries and sherry in a dish and allow to soak.

For the next layer, combine the milk, sugar and brandy in a double boiler and heat gently, stirring frequently. When hot, pour in the whisked egg yolks and continue to whisk until the mixture thickens. Pour this custard over the sponge mixture and prod the base with a knife to allow the custard to seep through. Allow to cool and set in the fridge.

The final layer is formed by spreading whipped cream over the custard and decorating the top with macaroons and chocolate flake.

# Walnut, Date and Fudge Flan

*Serves 8*

*Good Earth, Wells*
*Chef: Tina Dearling*

8 oz (225g) 100% wholewheat
   flour

4 oz (125g) butter
water to mix

*For the filling:*
8 oz (225g) muscovado sugar
4 oz (125g) walnuts, chopped

8 oz (225g) dates, chopped
½ pint (275ml) double cream

Rub the butter into the flour until it resembles breadcrumbs. Add water until you have a pliable dough. Roll out onto a floured board and line an 8" (20cm) flan case. Bake blind at 200°C/400°F/gas 6 for about 20 minutes until the pastry is crisp.

Place the sugar in a saucepan with a little water and melt over a low heat until it reaches the 'caramel' stage. Remove from the heat, stir in the cream, walnuts and dates. Return to the heat and boil for about another 2 minutes.

Pour the mixture into the flan case and allow to set. Serve with whipped or clotted cream. This flan is very rich and sticky so a small portion is quite ample.

# Super Natural Yoghurt

*Serves 4*

*Super Natural, Newcastle upon Tyne*
*Chef: James Leitch*

25 fl. oz (725ml) plain yoghurt
4 oz (125g) sultanas, washed
4 oz (125g) desiccated coconut,
    preferably coarse

juice 1 lemon

*Prepared in an instant, the unusual flavouring to this yoghurt makes it far superior to the bland manufactured varieties.*

Fold the coconut and sultanas into the yoghurt and add the lemon juice.

Leave for at least half an hour to allow the coconut to swell. Serve slightly chilled.

---

# Honey Apple Cake

*Serves 8–10*

*Season's Kitchen, Forest Row*
*Chef: Liz Boisseau*

8 oz (225g) margarine
12 oz (350g) self-raising flour
6 oz (175g) light soft brown sugar
1 teaspoon cinnamon
small teaspoon nutmeg

8 oz (225g) Cox's eating apples,
    peeled and chopped
4 oz (125g) raisins
3 eggs

*For the syrup:*
2 tablespoons honey
2 tablespoons apple concentrate

1½–2 tablespoons water

½ pint (275ml) whipped cream

good apricot jam to glaze

Rub the fat in the flour, add the sugar, spices, apple and raisins and then beat in the eggs. If you have a mixer, place all the ingredients in it and beat gently.

Prepare a 10–11" (24–26cm) ring mould. Place the sponge mixture in it and smooth over the top lightly. Bake at 180–190°C/350–375°F/gas 4–5 for 30–40 minutes.

Remove from the oven and cool the cake in the tin for about 15 minutes. During this time heat the honey, apple concentrate and water together in a pan until they form a smooth syrup. Spoon this syrup over the sponge and leave it to soak in. Allow to cool completely.

Carefully turn the ring out and cut in half horizontally. Sandwich the two halves back together with the whipped cream. Then brush the sponge all over with softened apricot jam, this gives an attractive glaze and a delicious flavour.

---

# Spicy Apple Cake

*Stanards, Canterbury*
*Chef: Jacky Luckhurst*

8 oz (225g) vegetable margarine
5 oz (150g) muscovado sugar or
 honey
4 eggs
8 oz (225g) 100% wholewheat
 flour

1 large eating apple, cored and
 sliced
1 heaped tablespoon mixed spice
2 oz (50g) flaked almonds

Cream the margarine and sugar together, then add the eggs and then the flour.

Place half the mixture in a greased and lined 9×4" (23×10cm) cake tin. Arrange the apple on top and sprinkle over the mixed spice. Spread the remaining cake mixture on top and sprinkle with flaked almonds.

Bake at 180°C/350°F/gas 4 for about 45 minutes until the top is firm and a knife inserted in the centre will come out cleanly.

---

# Banana Breadcake

*Food For Thought, London*
*Chef: Siriporn Duncan*

1 cup corn oil
3 cups soft brown sugar
1 cup milk with vanilla pod
2 cups mashed bananas
3 cups wholewheat flour
2 teaspoons bicarbonate of soda

2 teaspoons cinnamon
pinch ground cardamom
1 cup chopped walnuts
fresh cream, for decoration
sliced bananas, for decoration
chopped walnuts, for decoration

*If you can manage to resist the temptation, this cake is even better if allowed to mature for a day or two, stored in an airtight container. We have suggested you use cup measurements because we feel you should not be restricted by our measurements – so take your courage in one hand and a cup in the other and try this superb recipe.*

An hour before preparation, leave a vanilla pod to stand in the milk – the milk can be warmed slightly to increase the vanilla flavour but it must be cold before you start making the cake.

Blend the oil and sugar together in a separate bowl and then tip in the milk and mashed bananas.

Mix all the dry ingredients together in a separate bowl and tip into the liquid mixture. Beat thoroughly in a circular motion so as to beat in air.

Pour into a greased and lightly floured 1 lb (450g) loaf tin. Bake in a slow oven for 40–60 minutes – it takes a surprisingly long time to cook! When the breadcake is brown and risen, cover the top with foil to prevent it burning. It will probably take another 20 minutes to bake thoroughly. Remove from the oven and allow to cool completely before turning out.

Decorate with fresh cream and sliced bananas (previously sprinkled with lemon juice to prevent browning) and chopped walnuts. Or, more simply, just spread with butter.

---

# Bara Brith
*Serves 12*

*Siop Y Chwarel (The Quarry Shop), Machynlleth*
*Chefs: Anne Lowmass and Helen Allen*

8 oz (225g) currants
8 oz (225g) raisins
4 oz (125g) mixed peel
4 oz (125g) glacéed cherries
¾ pint (425ml) cold tea

1 lb (450g) wholemeal flour
4 teaspoons baking powder
6 oz (175g) muscovado sugar
1 egg

*We have adapted the traditional Welsh tea bread to produce this deliciously moist, rich cake.*

Soak the fruit in the tea overnight.

Add the other ingredients and mix to a stiff dough.

Pour into a greased 2 lb (1kg) loaf tin and bake at 180°C/350°F/gas 4 for about 2 hours, until the top is firm.

# Carob and Banana Cake

*York Wholefood Restaurant, York*
*Chef: Marion Hurley*

8 oz (225g) margarine
6–8 oz (175–225g) dark brown
   sugar, to taste
3 eggs

1 lb (450g) ripe bananas, mashed
2 oz (50g) carob flour
10 oz (275g) wholemeal flour
3 teaspoons baking powder

*Carob flour comes from the dried ground pod of the carob fruit, which is also known as Saint John's Bread as it is reputed to have sustained St John the Baptist in the Wilderness. It is dark brown, tastes like chocolate and can be used to make absolutely delicious cakes and desserts. It is naturally sweet and has less calories than cocoa! Unlike chocolate it is low in fat, is caffeine free and contains no theobromine. It is also a source of protein, calcium, the B vitamins and iron.*

Cream the fat and sugar and add the beaten eggs. Beat well – when using wholemeal flour in cakes, the more you beat the fat, sugar and eggs the lighter the cake will be!

Sieve the flour and baking powder together and add to the mashed bananas, mixing in well. Fold this mixture into the fat and sugar. The mixture should be of a soft dropping consistency. If necessary add a little milk to loosen the consistency.

Pour in a greased 7" (18cm) cake tin and bake at 180°C/350°F/gas 4 for about one hour or until a knife pushed into the top comes out clean.

Allow the cake to cool, remove from the tin and top with carob spread and slices of banana.

# Carrot Cake

*Nuthouse, London*
*Chefs: Abraham Nasr and Magdi Aboulnass*

5 oz (150g) oil or melted butter
4 tablespoons honey or raw cane
   sugar
10 oz (275g) wholewheat flour
2 eggs
1½ teaspoons baking powder

juice and freshly grated zest 2
   oranges and 1 lemon
½ teaspoon vanilla essence
4 oz (125g) carrot, grated
½ teaspoon cinnamon

*Dried fruit, such as sultanas or raisins can either be incorporated in the mixture or sprinkled over the top of the cake before cooking. This same recipe can be used to make an apple cake by substituting grated raw apple for the carrot.*

Mix the oil or butter with the honey or raw cane sugar. Add the flour, baking powder and eggs and beat well – preferably in an electric mixer.

Add the fruit juices, then the carrot and finally the grated zest and flavourings.

Pour into a greased ½ lb (225g) loaf tin and bake for about 45 minutes at 180°C/350°F/gas 4.

# Almond and Raisin Tart

*Herbs, Skipton*

8 oz (225g) wholemeal pastry
3 eggs
6 oz (175g) Barbados sugar
2oz (50g) plain flour

¾ teaspoon cinnamon
½ pint (275ml) natural yoghurt
4 oz (125g) seedless raisins
2 oz (50g) flaked almonds

Line an 11″ (28cm) flan ring with your pastry.

Whisk together the eggs and sugar until very thick. Mix together the flour and cinnamon and fold into the egg mixture along with the yoghurt.

Pour mixture into the flan ring and sprinkle with the raisins and flaked almonds. Bake at 190°C/375°F/gas 5 for 30–35 minutes or until a lovely golden brown.

You can serve this delicious tart hot or cold to preference.

---

# Lemon Spicy Cake

*Siwp Y Chwarel (The Quarry Shop), Machynlleth*
*Chef: Lyn Roberts*

6 oz (175g) sugar
6 oz (175g) margarine
4 oz (125g) wholemeal flour
4 oz (125g) porridge oats
½ teaspoon ground cinnamon
¼ teaspoon ground nutmeg

1 teaspoon baking powder
2 eggs, beaten
grated rind and juice 1 lemon
2 oz (50g) walnuts
milk to mix
4 oz (125g) soft brown sugar

*This is an unusual sponge mixture which uses both nuts and oats and is soaked in a lemon syrup which makes it very moist and extremely tasty.*

Cream together the sugar and margarine.

Mix the flour, oats, spices and baking powder together.

Add the flour mixture alternately with the eggs to the creamed sugar/ margarine to form a stiffish mixture. Add the lemon rind and nuts and a little milk if necessary if it is very firm. Spread the mixture into an oiled, shallow baking tin 7×10″ (18× cm) and bake for about 30 minutes at 180°C/350°F/gas 4 until the top is set and firm.

While it is baking, squeeze the lemon and mix the juice with the sugar.

When the cake is cooked, remove from the oven, pour the lemon syrup over the top and leave to cool. Cut into squares before serving.

---

# Tofu Cake                                              *Serves 6*

*Neal's Yard Bakery, London*
*Chef: Rachel Haigh*

*For the base:*
4 oz (100g) wholewheat flour
4 oz (100g) oats
pinch salt

2 fl. oz (50ml) malt
2 fl. oz (50ml) soya oil

*For the topping:*
12 oz (350g) tofu
½ pint (250ml) diluted apple
　concentrate or fruit juice
½ lemon, grated and juiced
3 tablespoons puréed dates or
　honey

1 teaspoon tahini (optional)
pinch mixed spice, nutmeg and
　cinnamon
fresh fruit to decorate

156

*This cake is our equivalent of a vegan cheesecake – no dairy or animal produce. It's also high in protein and low in calories!*

Make the base by placing the flour, oats and salt in a mixer and blend. Add the malt and mix well until evenly distributed and crumbly. Add the oil and press into an 8″ (20cm) circular cake tin. Bake at 170°C/325°F/gas 3 for 10–15 minutes.

Put all the ingredients for the topping into a blender and mix until smooth. Taste and add more lemon or sweetening as necessary. Pour the mixture over the partially cooked base and return to the oven for about 20 minutes or until the top has set.

Remove from the oven and leave to cool. Carefully remove the tin and decorate the top with fresh fruit.

---

# The Vegan (a chocolate cake with a difference!)

*Cherry Orchard, London*
*Chef: Michael Scherk*

*Dry ingredients:*
8 oz (225g) wholewheat pastry flour
6 oz (175g) brown sugar, with lumps broken up

3 rounded tablespoons cocoa, sifted
½ flat teaspoon salt
finely grated peel from 2 oranges

*Wet ingredients:*
5 tablespoons soya oil
2 tablespoons malt vinegar

1 teaspoon vanilla essence

9 fl. oz (250ml) cold water
½ rounded teaspoon baking

Oil and flour an 8" square baking tin.

Mix together well all the dry ingredients. Add all the wet ingredients and immediately pour in the water and beat thoroughly.

Just before baking add the baking powder and pour mixture into the tin. Place on the middle shelf at 170°C/325°F/gas 3 for 35–40 minutes.

Allow to cool for at least 1 hour before cutting. This cake will keep very well for several days in an airtight container.

Edinburgh

Newcastle-Upon-Tyne

Ambleside

Skipton    York

Manchester

Newark

Shrewsbury

Machynlleth

Birmingham    Cambridge    Ipswich

Llandrindod Wells

Crickhowell    Stroud    London

Bath    Croydon

Wells    Tunbridge Wells

Chichester    Forest Row

Castle Cary    Southsea    Eastbourne

Sherborne

Axminster

**Cheese Press** 18 High St, Crickhowell. (0873) 811122

**Cherry Orchard** 241 Globe Rd, London E2. 01-985 0641

**Clinchs Salad House** 14 Southgate, Chichester. (0243)788822

**Cranks** 8 Marshall St, London W1. 01-437 9431

**Country Kitchen** 59 Marmion Rd, Southsea. (0705) 811425

**Delany's** St Julian's Craft Centre, St Alkmund's Sq., Shrewsbury. (0743) 60602

**Diwana Bhel-Poori House** 121 Drummond St, London NW1. 01-387 5556

**Food For Health** 15/17 Blackfriars Lane, London EC4. 01-236 7001

**Food For Thought** 31 Neal St, Covent Garden, London WC2. 01-836 0239

**Food For Thought** Trendle St, Sherborne. (093 581) 4778

**Ganesha** 1 Western Parade, West St, Axminster. (0297) 33957

**Gannets** 35 Castlegate, Newark. (0636) 702066

**Good Earth** 4 Priory Rd, Wells. (0749) 78600

**Good Food Café** High St, Llandrindod Wells. (0597) 3320

**Grapevine** 2/3 Edgbaston Shopping Centre, Five Ways, Birmingham. (021) 454 0672

**Harvest** 29 Copthall Ave, London EC2. 01-628 6129

**Harvest** Compston Rd, Ambleside. (09663) 3151

**Healthy, Wealthy and Wise** 9 Soho St, London. 01-437 1835

**Henderson's Salad Table** 94 Hanover St, Edinburgh. (031) 225 3400

**Herbs** 10 High St, Skipton. (0756) 60619

**Hockneys** 96/98 High St, Croydon. 01-688 2899

**Huckleberry's** 34 Broad St, Bath. (0225) 64876

**Marno's** 14 St Nicholas St, Ipswich. (0473) 53106

**Mother Nature** 2 Bradford St, Stroud. (045 36) 78202

**Natural Snack** Community Health Foundation, 188/194 Old St, London EC1. 01-251 4076

**Nature's Way** 196 Terminus Rd, Eastbourne. (0323) 643211

**Neal's Yard Bakery** 6 Neal's Yard, London WC2. 01-836 5199

**Nettles** 6 St Edward's Passage, Cambridge. (0223) 59302

**Nuthouse** 26 Kingly St, London W1. 01-437 9471

**The Old Bakehouse** High St, Castle Cary. (0963) 50067

**On The Eighth Day** 109 Oxford Rd, Manchester. (061) 273 4878

**Pilgrims** 37 Mount Ephraim, Tunbridge Wells. (0892) 20341

**Siop Y Chwarel (The Quarry Shop)** 13 Heol Maengwyn, Machynlleth, Powys. (0654) 2624

**Season's Kitchen** Lewis Rd, Forest Row. (034 282) 3530

**Slenders** 41 Cathedral Place, Paternoster Sq., London EC4. 01-236 5974

**Super Natural** 2 Princess Sq., Newcastle upon Tyne. (0632) 612730

**Wholemeal Vegetarian Café** 1 Shrubbery Rd, Streatham, London. SW16 01-769 2423

**York Wholefood Restaurant** 98 Micklegate, York. (0904) 56804

# Index

# Index

## Fontana Paperbacks: Non-fiction

Fontana is a leading paperback publisher of non-fiction, both popular and academic. Below are some recent titles.

- ☐ CAPITALISM SINCE WORLD WAR II Philip Armstrong, Andrew Glyn and John Harrison £4.95
- ☐ ARISTOCRATS Robert Lacey £3.95
- ☐ PECULIAR PEOPLE Patrick Donovan £1.75
- ☐ A JOURNEY IN LADAKH Andrew Harvey £2.50
- ☐ ON THE PERIMETER Caroline Blackwood £1.95
- ☐ YOUNG CHILDREN LEARNING Barbara Tizard and Martin Hughes £2.95
- ☐ THE TRANQUILLIZER TRAP Joy Melville £1.95
- ☐ LIVING IN OVERDRIVE Clive Wood £2.50
- ☐ MIND AND MEDIA Patricia Marks Greenfield £2.50
- ☐ BETTER PROGRAMMING FOR YOUR COMMODORE 64 Henry Mullish and Dov Kruger £3.95
- ☐ NEW ADVENTURE SYSTEMS FOR THE SPECTRUM S. Robert Speel £3.95
- ☐ POLICEMAN'S PRELUDE Harry Cole £1.50
- ☐ SAS: THE JUNGLE FRONTIER Peter Dickens £2.50
- ☐ HOW TO WATCH CRICKET John Arlott £1.95
- ☐ SBS: THE INVISIBLE RAIDERS James Ladd £1.95
- ☐ THE NEW SOCIOLOGY OF MODERN BRITAIN Eric Butterworth and David Weir (eds.) £2.50
- ☐ BENNY John Burrowes £1.95
- ☐ ADORNO Martin Jay £2.50
- ☐ STRATEGY AND DIPLOMACY Paul Kennedy £3.95
- ☐ BEDSIDE SNOOKER Ray Reardon £2.95

You can buy Fontana paperbacks at your local bookshop or newsagent. Or you can order them from Fontana Paperbacks, Cash Sales Department, Box 29, Douglas, Isle of Man. Please send a cheque, postal or money order (not currency) worth the purchase price plus 15p per book for postage (maximum postage required is £3).

NAME (Block letters) _____

ADDRESS _____

_____

While every effort is made to keep prices low, it is sometimes necessary to increase prices at short notice. Fontana Paperbacks reserve the right to show new retail prices on covers which may differ from those previously advertised in the text or elsewhere.